More Praise

"Terrie Curry's personal story is part romance, part tragedy, and altogether inspiring. Through her whimsical and poignant writing, we are shown guideposts to help us through our own, personal challenges in life."
—Ashley Stamatinos

"Ms. Curry's experiences defy the mortal mind. She offers hope to all who care for an infirm or loved one that true life transcends the material body."
—Dottie Daves, CPA and CFO Federally Qualified Health Center

"*The Unspoken* is a genuine account of an exploration of consciousness and a guide post for anyone open to acknowledging the cues that spirit and communication exist on different levels. Terrie Curry gracefully writes about what many of us are uncomfortable addressing and inspires us to tune inward to fully connect ourselves to the Infinite, those we care about and the subtle world around us."
—Lisa Alvarez LAC, Founder of Healing Foundations Oriental Medicine and Acupuncture Clinic

THE
UNSPOKEN

It is entirely possible that behind the perception of our senses,
worlds are hidden of which we are unaware.
—Albert Einstein

Silence is potent....it lies beyond thought.
In silence one is in intimate contact with their surroundings.
It is, in short, transcendent speech or unspoken words.
—Ramana Maharshi

THE
UNSPOKEN

A Story of Love, Loss, and a
World Beyond Words

TERRIE C. CURRY

For more information contact:
www.terrieccurry.com
terrieccurry@gmail.com

978-0-692-65465-1 – paperback
978-0-692-65464-4 – eBook

Library of Congress Control Number: 2016903519

Book design by Dotti Albertine

Daddy, can you hear my mind?

Listen...it's talking in my head.

But we don't really have any minds.

We are pretending.

—Trystan (four years old)

———————

To Trystan—and children everywhere

CONTENTS

ACKNOWLEDGMENTS

A big thank you with all my love to Megan and Connor for the magic you have been in my life.

A heartfelt thank you to my sisters, my brother and all their spouses for being there for me: Especially M.B. for answering her phone at 2 a.m. on September 5th; Robbie for stepping in as midwife in the labor and birthing of this book; Pattie for her cheerfulness; and Joe for making me LMAO.

Thanks to Greg, for being Greg.

A special thank you to all my nieces and nephews for keeping me young at heart. I adore all of you!

Infinite gratitude for the mentors, yogis, and co-creators who have touched me personally, and contributed joyfully to every aspect of my life and living.

Immense gratitude to Jenny Sommerfield, my very patient and extremely talented editor; and to Michael Levin for his creative inspiration.

CHAPTER 1

Glimpsing a New Paradigm

I'm alive.

I can feel my heart beating. I can feel the pulse in my wrist. I'm alive—and so are you.

Beyond that, we have questions. How many of us find ourselves asking, *how* am I alive? What is my purpose, and does it end after my death? What *is* death? Where do we go when we die? And how are we all connected?

Today, in this new millennium, quantum science is revealing at warp speed that we are not separate individuals at all. We play a role, consciously or unconsciously, in a universe that is constructed of a vast field of information. We actually engage across time and space with the unseen energy of infinite possibilities.

Some quantum scientists are coming up with a "new" perspective, which is actually one that's been held by yogis and mystics throughout time. This scientific revolution began in earnest with astronaut Edgar Mitchell, the sixth man to walk on the moon. Mitchell, pilot of Apollo 14, had a simple but profound experience as he and his crew returned to Earth from the moon. Seeing Earth floating in the sheer vastness of space, he found himself engulfed in an expanded sense of universal connectedness.

It was an epiphany for Mitchell, and this moment in his life became the foundation on which he built the Institute of Noetic Sciences (IONS). In his words (http://noetic.org/about/history): "I realized that the story of ourselves as told by science—our cosmology, our religion—was incomplete and likely flawed. I recognized that the Newtonian idea of separate, independent, discreet things in the universe wasn't a fully accurate description. What was needed was a new story of who we are and what we are capable of becoming."

With the Institute, he shifted from operating as a strictly physical scientist—accustomed to directing his attention to the objective world "out there"—to a scientist investigating the nature of consciousness and recognizing the role it plays in human evolution.

Mitchell recognized that science might lead us to a different view of reality, where outer and inner are equal aspects in the miracle and mystery of being. And in writing my own story, I see how I have been riding the wave of this ongoing paradigm shift throughout my life.

In my early beginnings, as a young child, I was entrained with a Catholic concept of God and religion, and I had a devotional bent for saints and angels. My guardian angel sat on my shoulder protecting me. My patron saint, Therese of Lisieux, was my constant companion. I remember days that I'd forego recess at school, instead using my play time to pray to the Blessed Mother in the church next door. I begged and begged for the statue to talk to me as she had to the children of Fatima. But she never did. I never forgave her.

When I went to college, I explored philosophers like Sartre, Kierkegaard, Nietzsche, and others. An intellectual embracing of their work supported my choice to become agnostic. In spite of an academic stripping away of my belief system, I still imagined a Force that had birthed humanity. I still envisioned a unity throughout mankind, a womb of Oneness from which every race, creed, and color emerged. I had an insatiable curiosity about relating and communicating with this Force. I wanted to experience its Presence in my connection with others. Was it an outer Force I needed to reach out to? Or did the Force come from somewhere within?

In my early thirties, as I began to extend myself beyond agnosticism, the unknown became terrifying. I found myself in a deep, internal existential debate. This increasing struggle finally culminated in a lonely night of torment that I spent on the floor, wailing for God—any God—to resolve this conflict within me.

Similar to the conversations I had with Mother Mary so many years earlier, my pleading that night yielded nothing. I went to bed feeling exhausted and emotionally drained. But an event later the next day provided the "glimpse" I had been asking for.

It was evening, after the sun had set. I sat on the porch with my four-year-old son, Connor, watching the full moon rise on the horizon. We'd been playing our favorite game of listening to sounds and identifying them. On our list: #1, *crickets;* #2, *trucks on the highway;* #3, *an airplane overhead;* #4, *dogs barking.*

After sound #4, something shifted for me. I was no longer aware of the game we played, nor my son's presence on my lap, nor my place on the porch. Without moving, I somehow was being pulled toward the moon. The closer I felt, the bigger the moon became, until I was one with the moon.

Here, I felt a strong Presence, and waves of love flowed over me. My heart became tender. Even as my heart softened, reason and logic interfered, and I kept saying to myself, "I'm just in nature. This is just how it feels to be in the wild." Despite my efforts to discount what I was sensing, the Presence kept growing stronger and stronger. When I was fully engulfed in this Oneness, I ventured a question: "Is this really You?"

Then I heard Connor say, "#10 God." In that instant, I was back on the patio with Connor on my lap, counting the sounds he heard. He'd kept playing while I was disconnected from the game, and he was now on the tenth sound he'd heard. "Connor, what did you say?" I asked, shaken.

Without missing a beat, he said, "#10, *God.*" Matter-of-factly, as four-year-olds do, he said, "Mommy, God is talking to us." I looked at him in amazement and I felt instant gratitude.

For the next two days, I walked around in a state of peace and joy. Nothing irritated or disturbed me. I felt like I was the ocean, not just a wave; I was the flame, generating the heat. By the third day, this state of being had subsided, but the impact was firmly imprinted both in my heart and in my mind.

When I became a hospice volunteer, my ability to perceive beyond physicality—beyond my five senses—increased dramatically. Through observation, I saw mysterious things happen as people approached death. I became more adept at tapping into that subtle world beyond time and space. I listened to stories of near-death and out-of-body experiences. However, it was not until I met a seven-year-old named Alan—who, under the label of autism, showed me the vast, multi-prismed world that he and other non-verbal and energetically sensitive children experienced—that I truly saw life and beyond as a continuum. It started making sense that death could be just another possibility.

Whether or not we can see death's illusory nature, we yearn for that which is tangible. Even the most enlightened among us experience the grip death can have. In *Autobiography of a Yogi*, yogi Paramahansa Yogananda describes his reaction to receiving the news that his guru, Sri Yukteswar, had died: "Seething with rebellion, my soul was like a volcano. Beneath a hollow smile and a life of ceaseless activity, a stream of black brooding polluted the inner river of bliss which for so many years had meandered under the sands of my perceptions. Where has that divine sage gone?" Only when his guru materialized in front of him, a few months later with information about the worlds beyond did his bliss return.

In questioning the nature of death, it was actually the

experience I shared with my husband which enabled me to break through many of my long-held notions. Don was healthy and athletic, a vibrant man. Therefore, it came as a complete shock to suddenly find him in a coma. Everything happened so fast, there was no time to discuss what was taking place. A medically-induced coma meant that any form of traditional communication with him was not an option. I came face-to-face with the invisible as I listened within for information.

Was it intuition, or was it something more? Was it a sensing ability where I intermingled with Don and the Infinite Invisible in something that would remain unnamed and beyond description or definition? Was it resonance or a coherence Don and I had established between us that whispered guidance to me, moment by moment? Was it love?

Whatever "IT" was, it turned out to be an invaluable compass in our medical crisis. It became particularly important when I needed to advocate for him in the present-day western medical model, which does not value or possess a barometer for the extra-sensory world. Equally important was the feeling of connection with him that it provided throughout his hallucinations and cardiac arrest in ICU, his fourteen-day coma, five days of semi-verbal recovery, and the final hour when he transitioned.

It is no coincidence that I was born under the sign of Libra. My quest has always been to reconcile the disparate parts of me—the poetic versus the analytical. Frequently, I have found my desire for explanation bucking up against what my heart simply knows to be true. My experience with Don was like walking through fire. My rational mind became servant to my heart. As I watched what was happening around me, it became obvious that communication is not just what happens when you open your mouth and sound comes out. Our entire world is filled with information being transmitted and received, but many of us remain unconscious of what is being imparted. In this book, I will share with you my increasing awareness and fascination with this truth.

The story I will tell is a testament to my wonderful and loving partner; it is also a touchstone for anyone who is curious about the nature of consciousness.

Along with a tale of my spiritual journey, I will also offer practical tips on how to handle medical crises, and how to move through grief and sadness. I also will shed some light on navigating the modern medical system.

What I'd like for you to take away from my story is the inspiration and permission to acknowledge that when you tune in, you know what is best for you and your partner or loved one. The path to that inner knowing can be lonely and frightening. In this book, I hope you'll find some of the support you will need if you experience the physical loss of a loved one. This information can be a basis from which to access the courage you will need for your journey.

What is it that feeds the unwillingness to let someone go? Are we afraid of feeling responsible as we allow them to leave? Do we fear we won't have a reason to live once they are gone? Is there a belief that nothing else exists, so we hang onto them no matter what their quality of life? What can be done to prepare for illness or death?

With increased awareness around these questions, you will be better equipped to move beyond what appears to be a set of limited choices.

CHAPTER 2

Living (and Loving):
A Fifty-Something Romance

"**I'll give you** the skinny on *you*—but only if you give me the scoop on *me*." Don leaned forward over a table at Mama Thai's as he jokingly referred to the gossip he knew his best friend, Jon, was capable of. Jon had introduced us on a double date with him and his wife, Cassie, who was a dear friend of mine. As natural a matchmaker as a Jewish shadchan, Jon had delighted in delivering juicy tidbits to each of us before our first encounter. We were now on a date of our very own—and so began our fifty-something romance.

This time in my life was magical. My children were away at college and, after many years as a financial analyst, I'd decided to choose a career that opened up a deeper meaning in my life. First, I became a volunteer and then the coordinator of the vigil volunteer program at a local hospice. I was drawn to hospice not so much because I had an interest in death, but because of my interest in life. My desire to work with the dying was fueled by a fascination with the continuum of life and the possibilities that are available to us in the transition out of this physical form.

Prior to getting involved in the world of hospice care, I had become a fan of Elisabeth Kübler-Ross, the psychiatrist most famed for her books and workshops on death and dying. I was fascinated with her research on near-death experiences and the ability to connect with loved ones who have crossed over. Even as an M.D, rooted in logic and science, she was unafraid to include in her work the wacky world of the paranormal. What finally convinced me to serve in hospice care was Dannion Brinkley's, "Compassion in Action" workshop, which was a hospice training program based on his two profound near-death experiences.

While I was shifting from a career of cold logic and numbers to one of personal warmth and caring, Don was recovering from a failed second marriage. Don's second marriage had taken place rather quickly after the death of his first wife, Colleen. Grief from her death began to resurface after his sudden divorce from his second wife. Since I was involved with dying and bereavement, our conversations flowed with ease.

Colleen had been the love of his life, and he had taken care of her through a seven-year battle with brain cancer. In the end, after many tearful discussions with Don, she had made the choice to end aggressive treatment. Within three weeks of her decision, she died at home. Their final moment had come one evening while he was paying bills at the dining room table. He'd happened to glance over at her in her hospice bed, and in that moment she smiled at him and closed her eyes for the last time.

After Don talked about these intimate moments with me, our relationship flourished. He entered my active world of zany social workers and steadfast nurses. He was an immediate hit at our gatherings. As an ex-college basketball "leaper" and a polished IT executive, Don was an interesting character. He'd grown up in a small Ohio town identical to what he called "Andy Griffith's Mayberry," and he had a bit of a Mr. Rogers demeanor, even towering at six foot, three inches.

He was the type to happily disguise himself in a clever costume, whether at work, at a party, or just hanging out. I quickly got to know the Don dressed as an outlandish "flasher," complete with a trench coat that hid his fake "family jewels." I met the Don who transformed himself into a twisted rendition of Elvis. And I was introduced to a Don cloaked as Rodney Dangerfield's sadistic Dr. Vidiboombas. No holiday was required for such a display—he'd dress up any day, any time for the shock or giggle it might arouse. As the youngest of four boys, he was not at all self-conscious, and he thrived upon drawing attention to his antics.

Don's proclaimed perspective on life was that you should live it to the fullest, because on the day you die, you are gone—no continued consciousness, no spirit left roaming around the ethers. Since this is your one chance, he felt you should laugh a lot in the process. In this way, Don fit into my life with what I found to be an interesting paradox. With him around, I was able to work with my clients on the edge of death while still really embracing the humor in life.

Happy to have found each other, we moved into the next phase of our journey together. At age fifty-nine, Don realized that he was tired of life in IT, and he decided to retire early. We bought a condo in the trendy Old Town District of Lincoln Park, and we renovated the dismal 1970s-era space into a European minimalist sanctuary.

The garden was large and enviable by city standards, but it had been neglected. Don, a natural at growing things, made it his playground. Like an artist with his palette, he created anew: a redbud tree here, a Japanese maple there, and a voluptuous display of peach-colored tiger lilies, all of which delighted dog walkers and other passersby. Upon my request, he lovingly crafted a tulip bed of all red, telling me, "Those tulips are my legacy to you, Ter."

Don, simply put, was a joyful and energetic soul. If I was having a tough day facing a hospice case, I would hear him whistling while he cooked dinner and I would think to myself, "Really? What the hell is he so flippin' happy about?"

Even in his constant state of joy, Don was extremely perceptive. On my stressful days, he would pour me a glass of wine and bring it to me during my bath, or he would make a latte and show up with it when I was sitting at my desk. I marveled at the serendipity of finding such a generous and loving partner. What topped it all, however, was when he'd lie on my side of the bed to warm up the sheets on those cold Chicago nights before I came to bed. He was never trying to impress, please, or flatter me. His nurturing was so matter-of-fact—just Don being Don.

He was the same when people came to stay with us. He loved to serve others and care for their needs in a way that made them feel special. He had an ability to be interested in each person, no matter their age or status.

After we had lived together a year in the city, when the time was right in typical Don fashion—he asked my daughter Megan for my hand in marriage. He had an intuitive sense and, in his charming way, he knew how close she and I were. Rather than "claiming" me, he allowed her to hold the power to give permission. After she gave him the green light, he proposed to me during a romantic Valentine's Day dinner with a two-inch by two-inch fake diamond engagement ring. Costume jewelry was right in line with his sense of humor.

We had a simple wedding on our patio with a few friends and sages. The sage who spoke for the occasion was Balbir, a dear man from India to whom both Don and I had become close. I had met Balbir twenty years earlier, at a time when I was trying to integrate a passion for international finance with my deeper spiritual quest. He was a natural storyteller and his stories were magical, mystical, and profound. They always gave me glimpses of life's interconnectedness.

Balbir's own life story was intriguing. As a young boy, he had an unpleasant encounter with an occupying British soldier that shook him to the core. He was left rebelliously wondering, "What gives that soldier power over me?" Balbir had come to America at the age of twenty-two to attend college and immerse himself in the Western way of life. The philosophical question, "What makes some nations more powerful than others?" still lingered deeply in his being. In the 1970s, he became a highly sought-after international business consultant, and he traveled widely. He had found the "formula for power" and made it his own. He was on top of the world.

Then, at age forty, he had a dramatic spiritual awakening. He was on a business flight over the Mediterranean when he looked out of the airplane window and was struck by a thought: *If the Earth looks so small from a few miles up, how must it appear from a divine point of view?* Suddenly, he felt himself floating upward out of his seat—and out of the plane. As if in a dream, he traveled farther and farther away from the Earth, until it became a mere speck of dust floating in space. A voice out of nowhere asked him, "What do you see?" Images flooded his mind in rapid succession. His world travel experiences fell into dark contrast. He saw opulent riches and crushing poverty, wasteful gluttony and deadly hunger, extravagant revelry and hopeless despair. Then, just as suddenly, he was back in his seat as if nothing had happened.

After that flight, he started experiencing pain in his fingers. Over the following weeks, the pain spread throughout his body. For two years, he was unable to walk. Internally, he felt deeply torn—as if his world had been fractured in two. He was unable to reconcile the painful dichotomy he had been shown.

Doctors were unable to find a diagnosis for his ailment. Eventually, at the suggestion of his sister, he tried fasting. After five days without food and water, something happened: a vision came to him. Although he was unable to explain the vision in words, he had knowledge as to why he was here on Earth. At that moment, he knelt and dedicated the rest of his life to fighting world hunger. And, at that very moment, he suddenly was able to walk again.

Balbir proceeded to start a non-profit movement, Trees for Life, to empower the poorest of the poor to become self-sufficient. No longer seeking the source of power, he became plugged into that power. Over time, he had transformed into something of a legend for those who crossed his path—including Don.

Upon Don's first meeting with Balbir, after we had spent a casual evening together, Don patted him on the back and said, "Terrie told me you were an enlightened sage, but you're really just an ordinary guy!" Balbir threw his head back, laughing, and there was an instant bond. Of all the energy healers, mystical teachers, and shamans in my world, Balbir was the only one Don could actually relate to. That was why we chose to include him in our wedding.

Our handwritten wedding vows wove deeper threads into our relationship. Don was of the "from dust you are made and to dust you shall return" school and claimed to have no belief in anything beyond the physical world. But he was so excited when he delivered the following pledge to me:

Your friendship gives me peace,
I feel comfort from your companionship,
our love brings me joy,
I receive energy from your spirit.
I have come to value all of these gifts
more and more each day we are together,
And I dedicate myself to providing you
the same peace, comfort, joy, and energy
for all the time we have together
as two people and as we become one spirit.

He fulfilled the promise in his first paragraph during our four and a half years of marriage. I felt the second paragraph strongly in his passing.

My complementary promise to him was:

I promise to laugh with you, to cry with you,
to create, to express and to let my heart dance with you.
I will live on the edge with you until we ascend
into the unfathomable Universe of Universes.

His passing was what fully brought me against the edge of that unfathomable Universe, even while I was still clinging to the relative.

Don, being a logical math major, never quite bought into my exploration of the mystical during most of our marriage. He supported me but was unmovable in his belief that there simply was nothing else. Periodically, though, I would catch sight of receptivity in Don that indicated he was open to something greater.

A perfect example: Don had decided to visit a friend in Australia, but couldn't find his passport (he hadn't touched it in five years). It was getting closer and closer to the day of his departure, and we'd turned the condo upside down looking for the lost document, without success. In the car on our way to dinner one night, he finally appealed to me.

"Terrie," he asked, somewhat sheepishly, "you know all that stuff you do?"

I raised my eyebrows.

"Well ... I was wondering if you could do something about my passport."

I could tell this was rather difficult for him to explore, but I couldn't help but be amused. I cleared my throat. "So, are you asking me to tap into the Universe through question and intention? I thought you didn't believe in any of that!"

"Well, I just thought it's worth a try, since I can't find my passport anywhere ..."

I smiled a little. "Okay—but *only* if you admit that it's not a coincidence when you find your passport within twenty-four hours."

He hemmed and hawed, not sure if he could agree to that. Casually, I crossed my arms and said, "You should just call up and order another passport and pay the express charges."

"No, no," he said, "I'll go for it."

I couldn't keep the corners of my mouth from turning upwards.

That night, I asked the Universe to assist Don in connecting to his passport. Then I let go of it, because frankly, I really didn't care if he found it or not.

The next morning, Don came in as I was sipping my latte. "Ter," he said, "did you do anything ... you know, about my passport?"

All I said was, "Why?"

He joined me at the table and shared his story. In the dream he'd had the previous night, he was searching and searching for his passport, asking everyone he encountered if they'd seen it. Then a "being" (much to my amusement, he used this word) walked up to him and extended its hand to Don. When Don looked more closely, he saw his passport was in the being's outstretched hand.

Don said he had awakened with a start. His eyes were then drawn to the closet, and he saw that the door was ajar. As he took in the darkness, he saw an old briefcase leaning against the wall in the closet, and he somehow felt compelled to get out of bed and open up the briefcase. When he did, of course, there was the passport.

I playfully reminded him of his promise to acknowledge the quantum link between my request and the appearance of his lost passport, but he sort of laughed it off. Then I confided that I believe we all have these types of experiences, but some people pass them off as coincidence, while others realize a oneness, or unity. Obviously, his Australian friend was from the school of coincidence. After he told her how he'd found the passport, she stated that she didn't believe in such voodoo—but she was glad it had been found.

As our marriage continued to evolve and blossom, so did my newfound calling in hospice care. I asked Don once how he could appear so genuinely interested in people and what they had to say. At times, I found people exhausting—especially after an emotional day with my hospice patients. He answered matter-of-factly, "Well, I got that from Grandpa Corfman. He told me when I was a little boy that there's always something you can learn from every person you meet."

Well, I could sure see Grandpa Corfman's point of view, particularly when it came to my patients. Every one of them was unique, and Don was always willing to listen to my stories. For me, talking to my husband was a form of debriefing after tough cases, which hospice workers are encouraged to do with social workers on a regular basis.

One night, I got a call to go to a run-down nursing home to be with a forty-year-old man named Winston. I left the house and told Don not to wait up. When I arrived, I found the patient lying in his bed, naked and emaciated. His condition reminded me of the photos I had seen of concentration camp victims. In this case, however, his arms and legs were flailing uncontrollably.

This was my first experience with what I learned was Huntington's disease. Many of my patients were comatose, sleeping, or heavily sedated. Although Winston was unable to speak, make any sounds, or convey anything with gestures, he was alert. Our eyes immediately locked in communication with an electric intensity.

I put my hand on his heart and, for the next hour, I sang songs to him, silly songs I had sung as a child, maintaining eye contact all the while. When I leaned forward to stroke his face, I silently heard the words: " I-am-you, you-are-me." "Winston," I whispered, "you and I are one." Then I sat back with my hand touching his forehead, and for the next thirty minutes, I drifted into meditation. When I opened my eyes, Winston lay there in complete stillness. As my visit was ending, the nurse came in and informed me this kind of calm was unheard of with Huntington's.

I slowly gathered my things and went home. When I crawled into bed beside Don, I started weeping from a place deep inside. He sleepily put his arms around me and said, "Ter, is everything okay?" "Yes," I whispered back, grateful to have his strong, loving arms envelop me. A couple of days later, the hospice called to tell me that Winston had unexpectedly slumped over and died in his chair.

For the next few days, I kept seeing Winston's face and feeling his gaze. It was unusual, but I wanted to know more about this man. The hospice suggested I make a bereavement call to Winston's mother. A frail, old voice answered the phone. It was Helen. She had a raspy, Old World accent. At the same time, she sounded wise, gracious and accepting.

I told her I had spent time with her son and what a beautiful soul I felt he was. I let her know that, although we hadn't been able to communicate in words, I felt very close to him.

"Winston was noble and brilliant," she said quietly. Her tone was matter-of-fact, not like an overly proud mother. Her description of his brilliance caught me off guard. The fact was, while sitting with him, I wasn't sure if he could cognitively understand anything I was saying. When I pressed her for more information, she said, "Oh yes, Winston had an IQ of 160, and was a university professor."

She went on to tell me that he had just finished his Ph.D. in Theoretical Mathematics when he began having symptoms of Huntington's, a genetic disease. Like his deceased father, Winston's entire nervous system was affected by the disease, yet his intelligence was left intact. Helen explained that, although Winston was always considered to be an intellectual, he was a transcendentalist at heart.

During this short conversation, she and I felt a silent bond. I ended the call by expressing my gratitude for the intimacy she had shared, and she in turn acknowledged my kindness.

With every new hospice experience, I delved further into the study of meditation, energy healing, and mind/body awareness. My hospice patients were fertile ground for the practice of experiencing life at more and more subtle levels. It was like tuning into a sixth sense, so to speak. I was careful to just notice what I noticed. These were the stories I didn't mention to Don, because I wasn't sure his logical mind would really hear me.

Although Don did not appear to be on any kind of spiritual journey whatsoever, he had a pure heart and rarely judged people. I knew he was following a special path of his own. Often, I would tell him that he was probably already enlightened along with his "mystic" dog, Baron, who sensed Don approaching from five blocks away while waiting at the front door.

In my studies, I was always experimenting with some new lesson I had learned. A shaman taught me how to ease a soul's transition from the body by focusing on the flow of energy. As Mickey Singer explains in *The Untethered Soul*, this energy flow comes from the depth of our being, and has been called by many names. All the great spiritual traditions talk about spiritual energy; they just use different words to describe it. In Chinese medicine, it's referred to as *chi*. In the West, we call it Spirit. In yoga, it is known as Shakti. The body yoga centers where spiritual energy is concentrated are sometimes called "chakras."

We can use any words of description we want—the important thing to recognize is that we all feel the energy move at one time or another. That spiritual energy is what you experience when love overwhelms you. It is what wells up within you when you're excited about something. But when you feel hurt and close off your heart and mind, it is the power that lies dormant as all the light within you dims.

When spiritual energy is suppressed, there is nothing "flowing"—the energy is still present, but it can't get through. By working with points on the body and the chakras, it is possible to change and channel the energy flow. This can be done through words (mental or verbal), intention, movement, and touch.

I was given instructions by the shaman on how to brush over the body's energy centers, starting at the feet. I couldn't always "feel" the energy moving, but I knew from studying *Hands of Light* by Barbara Brennan that the energy centers were real. My intent was to allow the movement of the energy from the feet to the crown of the head, where the physical body's light "spirit" body exits. This practice, which the shaman referred to as "the boost," was easiest when I approached it with curiosity and a sense of discovery, rather than a results-oriented perspective.

One afternoon, Don dropped me off at an apartment high-rise to relieve a caregiver for a few hours. The patient, Gloria, was not imminent by hospice standards, but she'd been paralyzed by a stroke two years earlier and had spent the past year in a coma. So I thought I'd sit in the lobby and practice the boost for five minutes or so before I hopped on the elevator. I sat there and asked Gloria for permission to do the boost.

To enhance the "takeoff," I decided to pray to Mother Mary, whom I had loved as a child—but as I mentioned, I had become distanced from her. "Mother Mary," I said, "I don't know who you are, but some say you are a very loving energy. Please assist me in sending Gloria off on a more playful journey."

After practicing the boost in the lobby, I felt a little silly. I wasn't at all sure I would actually be confident enough to perform anything other than this dress rehearsal, but I headed to the patient's apartment anyway. When I knocked on the patient's door, the caregiver opened the door quietly and said, "Oh, I'm so sorry—she just passed away. But please, come in."

I felt a bit awkward, not quite knowing what my role was. I didn't want to be an imposition at this delicate moment. I respectfully went over to Gloria's bedside anyway. I gazed upon her now-serene face and was startled to see that there, beside her head on the pillow, rested a Catholic holy card of Mother Mary.

Two hours later, Don pulled up curbside next to the apartment building. "How did it go?" he asked when I got in. I wasn't sure what to tell him; once again, this was the kind of situation that he might attribute to coincidence, and I wasn't ready to have that conversation. So I just looked at him and smiled. He kissed my cheek, and we drove away.

CHAPTER 3

Playing with Alan:
An Overture to Awesomism

Even though I was absorbed in tending to the dying, an opportunity arose to become involved with children on the South Side. I had a friend who was a flamboyant second-grade teacher at Wilder Elementary School. She encouraged me to come assist her in the classroom a few hours a week, just for fun.

With the forewarning that Wilder was known as Chicago's dumping ground for behavioral problems and delayed learners, I volunteered to tutor reading. It didn't take long to see that these kids craved loving, undivided, one-on-one attention. They needed someone to reflect back to them that they were awesome! I filled that role easily, because I saw them as truly magnificent creators as well as proficient manipulators (like most kids their age).

There was Antoine, a bright-eyed child who carried a switchblade in his backpack to protect his grandfather on their walks to school. And Taurus was set to become the next Michael Jackson, moonwalking his way to the lunchroom. But it was Alan, a misunderstood seven-year-old diagnosed with autism, with whom I developed the strongest bond.

At the beginning of the school year, as I walked into the second-grade classroom, I asked myself a question: "Which child in this room could I connect with that would create the greatest possibility in the months ahead?"

As much as I wanted to assist these kids in expanding and growing, I wanted to learn from them as well. Children, in their unfiltered understanding of the world, can hold more insight than a person who has a lifetime of experience. Unlike adults, children are in a natural state of just "being" or "knowing." Rarely do they try to rationalize what they see or experience; they simply "go with the flow," happy when an adult adapts to their playful state of existence. The children I met in that classroom would indeed make it easier for me to tap into that space.

As I became involved with the class, I was given the nickname "Dr. Curry," a kind of female version of "Dr. Seuss." I enjoyed working with the kids and getting to know their personalities, but it wasn't until December that I really connected with Alan. I was at the school taking photos of the kids as we celebrated with a Christmas party. I had raised $500 to purchase party food and two simple gifts—colorful mittens and caps for each child, along with crazy rubber-band bracelets that were the rage at the time.

As I was taking pictures of the kids, I walked up to Alan, and a funny thing happened. When I looked through the camera lens to snap his picture, I saw a violet hue surrounding him and a ball of light in front of his face. I shook my head and shook the camera as if to shake away any delusions. Then I moved around, looking through the camera at various angles, trying to get rid of the image of light. Whatever angle I tried, the violet hue and the ball of light remained around Alan. *That's strange,* I thought, but I continued to snap away. When I looked at the photo later, the violet hue had disappeared, but the white ball of light remained.

Being part Puerto Rican and part white in the classroom of forty black children, Alan had a unique way of holding his own. When Taurus tormented him by calling him "white boy," Alan innocently said, "No, no, I'm not white, I'm mixed." For the most part, he seemed isolated from his classmates. When I was first told that Alan had been diagnosed with autism, I also learned that his mother had refused the diagnosis. Alan had therefore escaped the special ed classroom and was currently reading at the seventh-grade level.

At times, he could be uncompromising, and both the teacher and his mother found themselves dealing with full-blown temper tantrums. At home, beatings were common punishment. He was sometimes banned from reading books and going to his favorite place, the local library.

At the time, all I knew about autism was that Dustin Hoffman had played a cool role as an autistic character in the movie *Rainman.* The teacher may have known less than I did about the diagnosis; she told the other kids Alan was crazy and to treat him like a puppy dog. She liked Alan and felt it was in his best interest if his classmates left him alone. Alan couldn't have been more misunderstood. So I made a pact with the teacher to spend most of my time with Alan.

Soon after the Christmas party, I participated in a four-day workshop that had to do with cutting edge information on the evolution of consciousness. At the workshop, I heard of a woman named Suzy Miller with a program called "Awesomism." She was known for her unorthodox communication with non-verbal children diagnosed with autism, or children considered to be on the autism spectrum. I was told her methods were unconventional, and at the same time remarkably transformative. It was suggested she might be able to help me in my understanding of the ball of light and the violet hue I had seen surrounding Alan.

After sending Suzy a short email describing my situation, she responded with the suggestion it might be best to have a phone conversation. The following day, after I described my experience with Alan, she told me her story.

Suzy was a speech pathologist who had worked with thousands of children with delayed speech disorders. In 1999, while working with a four-year-old named Riley, she saw an opaque light form dangling above his head with a tail on it that went into his physical heart. The form was the exact shape and size of his physical body and was connected by a "cord" that hung off the light form's foot, went into the top of his head, and came to rest in his heart. This opaque form appeared to be barely attached to the boy's physical body.

Miller had a difficult time deciphering what she was seeing, because she had never experienced anything like this before. Riley communicated with her telepathically, letting her know what she could do to assist him. Although she didn't understand what she was seeing, nor what he was telling her to do, she let him take the lead. She soon learned the opaque form was a much lighter form called the "energy body," and that it was associated with the soul energy body.

This light body, or "soul body," is like a gridwork that supports the integration of the body, mind, and spirit, so they all are capable of functioning as one. In Riley's case, he was unable to integrate this grid-work into his physical body.

Suzy was confident that Alan, too, was "one of these kids" who were coming into the world with lighter frequencies as a catalyst or a call to change the planet. After incarnating, it was difficult for them to come all the way into their physical bodies because their human form was not a vibrational or energetic match for the energy of their souls.

These children are gifted with awesome abilities to perceive the world," she said. "I call it the oneness principle—the ability to be one with all things, to see across time and space."

Suzy finished our conversation with five pointers, which I wrote on a napkin:

1. Continue being fully present with Alan as you already are.

2. If you are present with him, he will trust you in a way he doesn't trust others.

3. Since you have bonded with him, he will communicate with you in ways you have never before imagined.

4. Through this bond with you, he will become more present with the teacher and the other children in his classroom.

5. He has most likely come to you for a piece of information.

Her insightful advice was fascinating, but I tucked the napkin into my pocket and didn't look at it again until the end of the school year.

Since my own children were now in their twenties, rather than being interested in changing the planet, I really just wanted to have fun with a seven-year-old. Alan and I had a blast together. Because he was so ostracized from his classmates, it was an easy transition to hanging out one-on-one. We even ate lunch in the classroom, away from the others. We fell into the habit of greeting each other with a handshake, a blink, or a hug—I always gave Alan the choice. This freedom was important because he didn't always want to be touched.

One day when I arrived, he was arguing adamantly with the teacher that his feet were frozen to the floor and he couldn't go to recess. She was all too happy to see me walk through the door. She threw up her hands and said, "I'm taking the other kids outside."

After we were left alone, I whipped out an imaginary hair dryer from my purse and said, "Alan, I think this will do the trick!" I showed him how to turn it on high and together we melted the ice around his shoes. Soon, grinning from ear to ear, he was good to go.

Another time, I found Alan walking around and bumping into things, proclaiming he was blind. I once again entered his world. Becoming blind, I started bumping into walls and chairs. He started giggling, and as his sight miraculously returned, he came to my rescue.

I shared these funny escapades with Don night after night as we dined and enjoyed Don's culinary creations. He grew fond of Alan and the kids just from the stories I told. Like my filtering of what showed up with hospice patients, I didn't tell Don about the violet hue and white light I had seen around this boy, nor anything about the conversation I had with Suzy Miller.

I was very happy when Don met Alan coincidentally one day and got to see the real kid, rather than just the caricature I had presented. When Don picked me up at the school in our Nissan Versa, three of the little boys, including Alan, helped me carry my things to the car. They were all eager to meet Dr. Curry's husband. And when they saw the car, they got very excited—not about Don, but about the car! I had to let them flop around in the back seat, pretending they were getting a cool ride. Don laughed and gave them all a high five as they ran off and returned to their classroom.

Along with the playful interactions with Alan, something else started occurring. He would "send me messages." These messages came at times when I was outside of typical waking consciousness. One time as I was falling asleep, Alan was there showing me a triangle he had drawn and colored in with a yellow marker. When I saw this image, I was overwhelmed with an immediate sense of peace and compassion. Another day, when I was meditating, I suddenly felt Alan's presence. Then, just like a mini-dream, I saw a quartz crystal shaped like a seven-carat diamond inside Alan's brain. A bright light was being emitted from the crystal. Alan reached into his brain and took a duplicate of the crystal and held it out to me. He asked, "Are you ready?"

I asked, "What is it?"

He repeated for a second time, "Are you ready?"

"What am I to do with it?" I asked.

Then, a third time, he said, "ARE YOU READY?"

My mind became a white slate and I said, "Yes!"

Then, in this vision, he placed the crystal inside my brain. In that moment of meditation, it felt like a light shot out in all directions from the crystal in my brain. I realized he was sharing with me, in metaphor, how he viewed the world from a vast, multifaceted prism—not from a single window pane or from a singular point of view. He was letting me know that, while I was helping him feel safe at school, he could teach, share, and show me things I had been heretofore unaware of.

At school, as Alan felt safer and more comfortable within his body, some of the boys asked to play with us. One day, Antoine and Taurus joined Alan in making a house and a lamppost out of clay. They rummaged around the closet and found some little plastic people to live in the house. Before I knew it, the three boys had their people huddling around the lamppost. There they were skillfully negotiating the sale of a "kilo of Colombian bam bam." The imaginary deal was pulled off smoothly, but the boys were most excited that none of their guys got shot.

After many months, Alan and I took a big step and decided to eat in the lunchroom. Alan picked a table in an isolated corner so we'd be alone. To my astonishment, one by one, every little boy from our class made his way to our table to eat with Alan and me. I could hardly wait to tell Don that night what had transpired. I relayed my story and I finished it with, "And the teacher was flabbergasted and said she has never seen such camaraderie between the kids and Alan."

Don started laughing and just shook his head. There was no doubt in my mind that, without the violet hue episode to confuse him, Don really got it—he could see the power in showing up and being present.

The end of the year rolled around, and it was announced that Alan's school was to be shut down and not reopened. Alan came to me and said, "I ask my mama for two dollars, one dollar for my lunch money and one dollar for you. But my mama said no."

I was surprised at his disappointment and replied, "Well Alan, it's okay, you don't owe me anything."

He looked down at his feet and said, "I know, Dr. Curry. I just wanted to give you a dollar because you've been so kind to me." My kindness had been returned a thousand fold by this brave and mighty little boy.

I had wanted to continue working with Alan over the summer, but it couldn't be arranged with Alan's mother. Don noticed my bit of sadness and said to me, "You have really become fond of that little guy haven't you?"

I thought, "Oh, if you only knew!"

In hindsight, it was fortuitous. That summer we became immersed with Don's health crisis. As school ended, I remembered the napkin I had stuffed away that had hinted of the future. I searched for it, mostly from a sense of curiosity. When I reread the napkin, I realized that everything Suzy had told me had taken place—yet my mind now wanted to attach a meaning to it all. When I called Suzy for some insight, she said, "I'm guessing Alan got the information he needed, and he was ready to move on."

My exchange with Alan empowered me to be confident in being present with those who could not verbally communicate with me. I became aware of the vast amount of information that can be shared in this manner and how accurate the information can be. I had begun interacting with Alan with the intention to have fun and help out—and yet, magical things had happened, things I couldn't explain.

From my hospice experience, I had learned that to simply sit and observe was a powerful practice. I had discovered that, if I could do that without thinking of why I was doing it and without trying to achieve a result, then what unfolded was always greater than anything I could have imagined. Playing and communicating with Alan was like upping the ante. I could see how we are all telepathically communicating all the time, but we trust the words we hear more than the non-verbal cues, which are actually more coherent.

Words slow everything down because they must come through a lens, so to speak, that "knowing" doesn't require. Using our energetic awareness of everything around us helps us open up to possibilities and therefore to a wider range of choices. When we go with our "knowing," then it's like possibilities move toward us. Words are an inadequate substitute for the actual awareness we are trying to describe.

With Alan, I had to pay particular attention to whatever my rational mind tried to "shoot down." I had to be open to whatever presented itself in our relationship. Whenever I was in a state of allowance and curiosity with Alan, more insight into this alternative experience of consciousness appeared.

Learning the authenticity of non-verbal communication through my interaction with Alan proved to be critical in my ability to assist Don in the days to come.

CHAPTER 4

"Expert Advice"

It would have been obvious to even the most casual observer that Don and I absolutely loved Chicago. Simply flying into Midway after jaunts to other places always felt good. Chicago was home for us. Heading toward the city on Lake Shore Drive and coming up onto the sight of Buckingham Fountain and the spectacular Chicago skyline was a thrill. Don would get a big smile on his face and say, "Look, Ter! Ya gotta love this city!" However, we were also aware of Chicago's dark side. The depth of the gangs, drugs, and violence in the inner city was legendary.

As I worked at the elementary school, Don channeled his strapping good health and natural athleticism into a similar pursuit. He had an old basketball buddy who coaxed him into helping coach basketball and tutor math at Faith Academy, a school based in a Christian philosophy. (Naturally, Don found humor in the fact that someone on the staff was always trying their best to convert him, since he wasn't religious.)

The academy was housed in an old formerly Catholic school building adjacent to a very rough neighborhood. It was supported by private funding, which the founders solicited in order to supplement tuition. Kids in the inner city found in Faith Academy a haven from gang pressure and bullying, both of which were rampant in the public schools.

The school had trouble with a constant turnover of staff, and Don became a reliable, stable symbol for these kids, many of whom had turbulent home lives. The basketball players grew to admire Don, knowing he was always there for them. He put them at ease, and the boys reveled in his kidding. One of the players, Tyrone, had a reputation of being afraid to shoot the ball, so Don chided him in practice. Finally, during a game, Tyrone dribbled and pulled up for a jump shot. With a wide grin, Don immediately yelled from the sidelines, "Tyrone, do you know that was a jump shot you just took?" Later, Tyrone told him, "Mr. C, I wanted to laugh, but I knew I was on the court and I had to stay focused." Don's encouragement, combined with his sense of humor, often had a sweet effect on the players' confidence.

Don's boys were protective of him. One winter evening after basketball practice, the boys watched Don walk to the bus stop in the dark to catch a ride at 16th and Pulaski. "Hey, Mr. C, what d'ya think you're doin'?" one kid asked. "Don't walk alone in the dark. Guys like us are just waitin' to jump a guy like you." Now granted, Don had silver hair and was lanky, but even at age sixty-two, he was still a presence on the court. He had naively figured he was also a presence on the streets. This was a gentle wakeup call from these kids who knew this old guy would be seen as an easy target.

For Don, who had never been the victim of an act of street violence, the boys were instrumental in opening his eyes to their world. One day, Cortez, one of his team members, came to practice with his foot wrapped up. He was sitting on the bench and, in his usual fashion, Don started teasing him a bit. Pointing to the injured foot, Don jovially asked, "What happened there, big guy?"

Cortez, acting nonchalant, told Don that over the weekend a gang member had held a gun to his head. Fortunately, at the last minute, they had decided to spare him and shot him in the foot instead. It seemed on the surface as though Cortez just took it in stride, a way of life that he had surrendered to. Yet Don was aware that, despite all the fear and anger that Cortez and the rest of the guys pushed down deep inside, the basketball court was a safe place and a constructive outlet.

Although Don could feel the singe of violence and saw how death lurked in front of these kids, he knew that for the two of us, that danger was still at arm's length. In light of the threat they lived with, we found it touching that chocolate chip cookies made from scratch (my simple contribution to the team) could bring the broadest of smiles to the players' faces. Don got such a kick when Willie, the leading forward on varsity, would cajole him: "Mr. C, when is your wife gonna make us some more of those cookies? They are the best!"

Such was our vibrant affection for the South Side. Don's ability to be active in sports and involved with the kids was based on the fact he was a healthy guy. He expected to live until he was ninety, just like his Grandpa Corfman.

Don believed in traditional medicine, but over time, he also began to appreciate the value of the holistic approach. When his internist diagnosed high cholesterol and prescribed some medication, Don chose instead to stop eating his beloved Chicago-style hot dogs. He took Red Yeast Rice supplements instead of Lipitor. By adding regular acupuncture treatments as well, Don lowered his cholesterol by more than 25 percent, putting him well into the healthy range. The doctor who had scoffed at Don's initial strategy was surprised when he observed the results. Don was a happy camper because he had formerly experienced adverse effects from even the mildest painkillers like Vicodin. He knew he just didn't do well on drugs.

Surprisingly enough, the real scare came not on the South Side of Chicago, nor during regular visits to his doctor, but on his trip to Australia. Don had an episode of atrial fibrillation, or A-fib, meaning his heart wouldn't beat in a normal rhythm. This put a little blip in his lifelong stretch of A-plus scores in health. One of the Australian friends he was visiting, who happened to be a doctor, informed Don that he needed to be on Coumadin, a blood thinner, to avoid stroke. Furthermore, he should consider an ablation to fix the heart flutter. In fact, the doctor recommended a world-renowned cardiologist, Dr. Whitmore, who just happened to be practicing in Chicago.

Don arrived home from his trip restless and worried. With my encouragement, he proceeded to obtain two very diverse medical opinions. Then an inner struggle emerged.

Dr. Whitmore was famous for being the wizard of the ablation procedure. He was in his fifties and highly sought-after, with a very busy calendar. Within thirty minutes after we entered his office, he calmly told us that Don would never cure his atrial fibrillation without drugs and/or an ablation. When Don, who was still reluctant to take drugs, interjected that we appreciated his opinion, Dr. Whitmore said flatly, "This is not an opinion. This is scientific fact."

The doctor smugly told us that the success rate of an ablation was around 60 percent, and he proceeded to describe the cocktail of drugs that would be required along with the procedure. He ended the appointment by informing us that eventually, the A-fib would put Don at serious risk of stroke. If he was interested, Don needed to get on Dr. Whitmore's calendar as soon as possible.

As we left the doctor's office, it occurred to me that this man lived in a paradigm which excluded a range of possibilities outside his medical model. With thirty years of focus and concentration already under his belt, it was doubtful that he would be willing or even capable of expanding beyond it. We needed a second opinion.

After some research, we chose Dr. Faraday, an alternative doctor who was a brilliant throwback from the sixties. He was approaching age seventy and hadn't let the standard medical model tarnish his care for patients nor his ethics in medicine. At their first meeting, he and Don laughed together after discovering they shared a mutual 1960s' fetish for Harley motorcycles. After swapping a few stories about their road trips, they moved into a discussion of Don's health.

First, Dr. Faraday said he believed Don was not at risk for stroke, because his tests showed a low $CHADS_2$ score, the standard clinical measurement for estimating the risk of stroke in A-fib patients. Furthermore, Don's lab results showed he had an autoimmune thyroiditis, which Dr. Faraday said is often related to A-fib. Eager to get his take on it, Don brought up the possibility of the ablation procedure. Dr. Faraday replied, "If they are suggesting an ablation, run as fast as you can in the opposite direction."

"C'mon," Don insisted, "a renowned specialist who has expertise in this area must certainly know more than you or me when it comes to correcting my condition."

Dr. Faraday just shook his head and said, "The specialists are compromising healthcare. Insurance companies are essentially rewarding doctors to do major procedures even when something less invasive is more appropriate." He went on to explain how medical research studies can be skewed to come up with data that supports a desired conclusion, and he said the success rates rarely include a follow-up period after the procedures have been performed. He pointed out that many patients who make it through the surgery may develop problems afterwards. We concluded the appointment, and as Don shook his hand, Dr. Faraday kindly reminded us that people can live a long time with A-fib.

In reviewing Don's choices with him, I discovered that,

although he was frustrated with the subtle flutter he was experiencing, he found the touted "risk of stroke" to be far more worrisome. He was leaning toward having an ablation. I reminded him of his low CHADS$_2$ score, which indicated a negligible risk of stroke. Then I mentioned that even his acupuncturist had verified that he served patients much younger than Don who had learned to live with the subtle flutter.

Still, after weighing his choices, Don ended up convinced that the advice of Dr. Whitmore, the "expert," was golden. He was optimistic that the procedure would work and he was looking forward to being back in the saddle (or at least, back on the golf course) within a few weeks.

Three hours after the procedure began, on Friday, July 7, Don came through with flying colors, literally—his torso and groin were massively bruised with a deep purple and blackish blue. I later found out that this type of bruising was a red flag for internal bleeding, which was a risk of the Coumadin blood thinner.

When he was released from the hospital, the true journey began. Over a two-month period, severe side effects started to creep in: headaches, fever, nausea, chest pains, blurred vision, and dark urine. I suspected that Don's required drug regimen might be creating some of his symptoms, but I was out of my element.

Don quickly became depressed and had trouble sleeping. One night, he turned to me and said, "Ter, what's wrong with me?" For the first time, he asked me to do some energy work on him, and I agreed. When I held my hands two inches from his chest, I felt strong heat radiating from his body. It felt like the blistering heat coming off of the pavement on a hot, summer day. The energy work helped him to relax for the evening, and he soon fell asleep.

The next day, we went to see Dr. Whitmore. The surgeon mentioned that Don had a small build-up of blood around his heart, but he seemed unalarmed and told us that his symptoms were normal. Later in the week, Don's fever reached 102 degrees. He called Dr. Whitmore for a phone consultation, and the doctor prescribed an intense dose of Ibuprofen, along with the Coumadin he was already taking. However, the anti-inflammatory failed to impact the fever.

At 9:30 p.m. on Friday, September 2, I went to the airport to pick up Connor, the son who had so poignantly identified God at age four. We were headed home on the Stevenson/I-55 when I got a call from Don. I heard him say weakly, "Ter, I'm passing out"—and then, to my horror, the phone went dead. I tried frantically to call him back, but Connor, ever the voice of reason, yelled, "Mom, Mom … call 911!" I tried to breathe and called 911 as we sped down the highway.

Within ten minutes, we were home. The ambulance had already arrived and the EMTs had broken down the door to find Don semi-conscious and turning blue. I rode to the hospital in the ambulance with him. By the time we reached the emergency room, his vital signs had stabilized and Don was alert and conscious. He admitted to me that he was afraid, and he got choked up as he told me why.

"Ter, I keep feeling like I am going to pass out when I lie down, and I'm afraid that I won't wake up." I felt for Don, but I wasn't as worried; I really thought everything would be okay. After all, he didn't have a terminal disease. There wasn't anything life-threatening here, or so I thought.

Don was admitted to the hospital and we were notified that his surgeon was assigning his partner, Dr. Locke, to follow up on Don's situation in the morning. The next morning, though, there was no Dr. Locke. We continued waiting for thirty long hours, and while Don was able to pass the time patiently, I was beside myself, rattling cages with nurses to hunt down the cardiologist.

During the wait, Don continued having cycles of fainting. Finally, a concerned internist made the decision to move Don to ICU. The internist, abiding by standard ICU protocol, asked Don if he wanted life support and life-prolonging measures in case of an emergency. I didn't think much of it. Don brushed the question off, too—after all, it was standard procedure—and said, "My wife has my power of attorney, so just consult with her if need be."

Don finally got settled in at about one in the morning, and I decided to go home and let the dog out. The ICU technician said, "Ma'am, do yourself a favor and stay home tonight and get some sleep. Your husband is in good hands." Don smiled ever so sweetly and said, "Yeah, Ter. Really, I will be okay. You need some sleep." Still unaware that Don was in real danger, I just laughed a little. No matter what, I wasn't willing to leave him alone for too long. I told him, "Oh no, I will be back in thirty minutes, my dear!" I kissed him and squeezed his hand before walking out the door.

When I returned, the technician was sitting at his desk outside Don's door, doing paperwork. I walked past him into Don's room and immediately panicked when I found Don thrashing and saying outlandish things. At that point, the reality that we were in crisis hit home. I kicked into gear and ran into the hall, and the craziness began.

"What is going on? What did you give him?" I yelled at the technician.

Nonplussed, he asked, "What do you mean?"

"My husband is hallucinating!" I retorted.

"How do you know?"

This was too much. I came unglued. "Because he's muttering bizarre things like he has to get up and go to the bank!"

The technician responded by walking up to Don's bed and saying sternly, "Mr. Corfman, please stop trying to get out of bed, or we will have to restrain you." In response, Don's eyes looked like a wild horse's, and he became even more stressed out. I stood by the bed and said firmly to the technician, "You *will not* restrain him. I will stay here and keep him from getting out of bed." The man just looked at me and left the room to fetch additional staff.

For the next thirty minutes, I kept my eyes on Don as people in blue scrubs started filling the room. They were all concerned with the monitors. While looking into Don's eyes, I could feel a dread rising in me. I started sensing something. *Oh my God,* I thought in a panic, *he can't breathe.* I screamed, "He is suffocating. Lift his head! Do something!"

It was too late. I felt alone and helpless as I watched Don's eyes become vacant. It was like a candle had been snuffed out. His eyes remained open as a single tear rolled down his cheek, but I knew he was gone. In that moment, time stood still. I felt like I was sinking. Then I heard a doctor yell, "Get her out of here."

Someone dragged me from the room and sat me down at a desk. The terror of what I had just seen coursed through my body. There I was, by myself, with my head in my hands. I was unable to process thoughts. Instead I wailed senselessly.

Over an hour later, someone finally tapped my shoulder and said, "Dr. Locke is ready to see you." Ironically, the doctor who had been so difficult to locate, had now worked on Don for more than thirty minutes to restart his heart, and I found myself in his arms as I sobbed uncontrollably.

After graciously allowing me that, Dr. Locke gave me the news that Don had flat-lined and was now in an induced hypothermic coma. They would keep him "frozen" for five days, trying to save his brain. Of course, there were no guarantees. He took time to tell me he suspected the cause was infectious rather than cardiac. He never told me what really happened, and after expressing his empathy, I never saw Dr. Locke again. I had never felt more alone.

CHAPTER 5

Difficult Choices

When the nurse led me in to see Don for the first time, his body was lying there, motionless and bloated. He was pumped with a whopping 3770 mcg of Fentanyl, a heavy-duty narcotic. Sam, a charming young resident who had befriended me in the crisis, stood beside me, and he admitted this was a record dose for what he had seen in his young career. I placed Don's hand in mine. It was cold, very cold. This was testimony to the initial five days of hypothermia, the protocol of choice.

Cold water immersion experiments had been known to slow down cellular respiration, putting the body in a state of stasis. In Don's case, all organs had failed; the hypothermia was an attempt to save his brain from more damage, since less oxygen would be required. As I looked at him, an image of the warm, brief kiss we had shared less than five hours earlier swept through my mind and tugged at my heart.

My two children soon arrived, and we set up camp in the waiting room. This was to be our home for the next ten days. Meanwhile, Don's case was the buzz of the ICU. Brain, kidney, cardiology, infectious diseases … it was like an organic laboratory for interns. As they traipsed through in groups, trying their best to be respectful, there was something there for all of them to learn.

In the background, my daughter Megan and I were more interested in our own "energetic laboratory." Megan had previously become a certified facilitator in an energetic transformation program called ACCESS Consciousness. She helped me review how to best apply this system, which entailed using specific verbal processes and hands-on bodywork to unlock tension, resistance, and dis-ease in the body. The founder had taught her well, and she had witnessed amazing transformations. For me, not much incentive was required, based on the grim circumstances we were facing.

Once again, I found myself experimenting with life's mysteries, but this time with my husband. I had no doubt that, as vibrational beings, our words and the ACCESS verbal processes carried potency. But I knew the first caveat was for me to be willing to let Don stay or go. This was reiterated in my phone call to the "Wise One," our friend, Balbir.

During these first few chaotic days, Connor handled most of the phone calls from concerned friends and family, but I wanted to personally make the call to Balbir. He picked up on the first ring, and his voice with its lilting Indian accent was such a comfort to me.

"Terrie," he said compassionately, "know that Treva and I are always here for you. I will pray, and you must keep your mind in a state of calm as best you can. As you sit by Don's bedside, keep emotion at bay as much as you are able. Think of him in a state of peace. You are now his only connection to the earth. And after what he has been through, he will now be asked one question: Do you want to go or do you want to stay? And if he chooses to stay, he will stay to bring or teach something to mankind—a mission, if you will. Yet if you try to hold him here against his will, by pulling on him emotionally and mentally, it will be tragic for him and for you and for all those around him." Balbir told me he loved both Don and me, and we hung up.

With Balbir's words to bolster me, I was ready for the work ahead. As we readied ourselves beside Don's bed, Megan told me she would put her hands on Don's head while I held his feet. This process would energetically reconnect Don to be in communion with the earth as his body released any resistance or shock for being here. Then an integration phase would unfold. Full integration, or the body's intelligent ability to stay or leave, would eventually require his being "unplugged" from artificial support.

"Mom, are you in?" Megan asked. I nodded.

Megan asked the energy to run, and then we asked in tandem for his body and being to be in communion with the earth. After a few minutes, Megan felt heat coming from Don's frozen head, and under my hands, I felt something like a sheet of ice cracking at his feet. The monitors started going haywire, lighting up and beeping. A nurse who heard the chaos ran into the room and, after glancing at the monitors, she gave us a look of surprise. Then she shooed us out. Megan smiled at me as we moved quietly out of the way. It would be days before our work showed its true potency.

I had started sleeping on a cot next to Don's bed so he would know I was there. Even though I was getting very little rest, I was vigilant every step of the way to avoid drifting into auto-pilot and letting the doctors or staff control our choices.

It was our sixth day of the coma, and the thawing process had just begun. After his examination of Don, the neurologist, Dr. Hawking, informed me that Don's brain didn't look healthy. He said there was a delayed effect from hypothermia and the huge doses of medications. If the brain stem had been damaged—as he believed it had—Don would not be functional.

He recommended three days of dialysis—ample time to clear the toxins, if the kidneys were going to respond. If Don's kidneys cleared, he advised, we would want to see him awake with open eyes, reacting to his environment by recognizing and communicating with loved ones. We essentially needed to see that someone was "home."

After three days, there was only a trickle of urine passing into the urine bag, and Don now had liters upon liters that needed to be released. His platelets plummeted to dangerous levels due to a side effect of a massive dose of Heparin. The dialysis was terminated. His renal failure had not been reversed.

The neurologist, Dr. Hawking, admitted to me that, despite all of our scientific and technological advancements, very little is known about the brain. He told me that, in his opinion, MRIs and scans are not always useful, and one must rely on the reactions and recovery of the patient to discern damage to the brain.

Dr. Hawking told me gently that Don's current responses were not from the intelligent part of the brain—they were mere responses from the damaged brain stem. He suspected Don had "locked-in syndrome," a condition I had briefly heard of. He warned us to distinguish between nervous system responses and signs of real intelligence. The left toe twitching, a right finger moving, his eyes blinking—in Don's case, these were all just nervous system responses that gave no indication whether his intelligence would come back.

But when I talked to Dr. Shepard, the head of ICU, I was perplexed by the mixed messages I received. I became aware of an uncomfortable dichotomy. Dr. Shepard interpreted Don's success in neurological function as a quantum leap. He got excited as he painted a rosy picture of Don's recovery, due to his recent nervous system responses. When I confronted him with the information I had received from Dr. Hawking that very little is known about the brain and we were seeing no real improvement—Dr. Shepard looked disturbed and said he would talk to Dr. Hawking.

I was getting closer and closer to moving Don into hospice, and yet the hospital was talking more and more about the need for a feeding tube. There was no discussion of taking him off the ventilator. The subject of a long-term prognosis was kept at bay. Each team of doctors talked more and more about bringing in different neurological experts. What I was hearing was, "keep him alive at all cost."

It was at this point that my eldest sister, Mary Beth, arrived from Minnesota. She had been a lobbyist in Washington, D.C. for healthcare providers, and I was eager to have her review Don's health insurance policy. At this point, I had no clue as to the extent of Don's medical coverage. After looking at Don's policy, she was aghast. "He has the best insurance parameters I have ever seen. Ter, there is no cap to his coverage." For the organic lab, it was *carte blanche.*

I arranged a meeting with Dr. Shepard and informed him I was leaning toward bringing in hospice. He tried to discourage me, and finally told me that since they were a Catholic hospital, pulling all the plugs and ending aggressive treatment was against their policy. Don would have to be moved elsewhere.

However, there was one internist, Dr. Singh, who was forthright. One day, standing in the hallway with me, he quickly ended all confusion and intrigue as to why Don flat-lined. It reminded me of the unraveling of the mystery in a "whodunit" play. Dr. Singh explained the following: Lab reports had ruled out infection and confirmed it was a cardiac issue. Two liters of excess blood trapped in the heart sac had put pressure on the heart, causing cardiac arrest. Coumadin and Ibuprofen, commonly known to be a dangerous combination, were the likely culprits of the buildup of fluid. Don's cardiologists had failed, for whatever reason, to respond appropriately and in a timely manner.

I now knew why I had such a strong sense that Don couldn't breathe when he coded. His brain was actually suffocating from lack of oxygen as his heart malfunctioned.

When I asked for Dr. Singh's advice about Don's current status, he told me that, aside from a spontaneous miracle, Don's prognosis would be a long life in a nursing home bed. Furthermore, even if Don showed some recovery, it would be a laborious process, as every organ had been grossly damaged. He made the point that someone younger might have an easier time making a comeback.

I had the feeling Dr. Singh could acknowledge and honor a greater range of choices because he came from a different paradigm. He didn't appear to have a fixed idea on what I should do, and he was interested in quality of life. He promised me that, whatever I decided, he would assist me.

Dr. Singh let me know that he was willing to make arrangements for Don to be transferred to the inpatient hospice wing at St. Germain Hospital, at my request. He said he believed this was the highest quality option for end-of-life care.

That night, I sat beside Don, holding the power of attorney document in my hands. Don had now been in a coma for fourteen days. He appeared to be in a vegetative state. As I began to grasp this whole scene, it brought back memories of my hospice experiences. Images flashed through my mind of nursing home patients who were near comatose, demented, and hooked up to feeding tubes or being force-fed. One woman, aged ninety-two, had wanted to die so badly that she had refused to open her mouth, triumphantly starving herself to death. I held the hand of Anna, a different woman who was blind and suffered from congestive heart failure, who had no known relatives alive. I whispered in her ear, "Anna, how can I help you?" With all her strength, she had pulled herself up and whispered in desperation, "Please help me die quickly." Another woman had lain in a coma for ten years, connected to a machine, because her son loved her so much that he didn't want her to go.

And finally, I thought of a woman in her sixties whose husband was forcing her to eat as she wasted away from cancer. When I entered the room, she was wailing, "Dear God, dear God, don't make me eat. Please, please let me die. " And then, of course, there was Don's late wife, Colleen, whose choice to end aggressive treatment at age forty-two Don had honored so courageously.

As I glanced at the document, I felt the irony that the legal words were in black and white while the situation itself was in shades of gray. I turned to the second page, and there was Don's confirmation, where he had initialed his choice:

I do not want my life to be prolonged nor do I want life-sustaining treatment if my agent believes the burdens outweigh the expected benefits.

I want my agent to consider the relief of suffering, the expense involved, and the quality as well as the possible extension of my life in making decisions concerning life-sustaining treatment.

Tears welled up within me, when I reviewed the meaning

of "relief of suffering" and "quality of life." But the real key for me was that I felt the life support—the work of medicine and machines—had plateaued in their ability to assist him. I felt that the intelligence of his body needed space to regenerate. And I had seen more than one case in hospice where patients had rebounded and started the actual process of healing once removed from machines and ICU.

As I looked at Don's signature on the last page, I could feel him, his essence, in the handwritten scribble. The next day, with a sense of peace, I asked Dr. Singh to arrange for Don's transfer to the palliative care unit at St. Germain.

CHAPTER 6

Beauty in Reconnecting—
Grace in Passing

With Don now in hospice, we had a change of guard. My daughter and son headed back to their jobs in Kansas City and Boston. My three sisters showed up, one by one, as fresh recruits. The hospice ward was a quiet enclave in comparison to the noise and intensity of ICU. It was easy for my sisters and me to hold a vigil of meditation 'round the clock at Don's bedside. The nurses commented on how peaceful it felt to be in his room.

Within the first forty-eight hours, Don's kidneys, which had so stubbornly resisted dialysis, kicked in and started releasing urine. Aides had to scurry to keep the bag drained. With the clearing of the toxins over the next few days, something unexpected and very strange happened. Don's eyes opened wide, bug-like, while he simultaneously made bird-like sounds: "Kah, kah ... koo, koo!" He had no recognition of me or anyone else, and his stare was blank. Trying to connect with him was like talking to a lunatic. This frightened me. I had never experienced anything like it. I kept thinking, "This isn't the Don I know."

After sitting with Don in this condition, rather than thinking he had gone insane, I tapped into something else I had previously heard can occur during the dying process. An energy healer had once explained to me that sometimes when a person dies their energy light body can become lost as they exit the dense, physical body. (I imagined it to be something like what was portrayed in the movie "The Sixth Sense.") According to her, when this happens instead of moving on, the lost being is drawn to look for another physical body to inhabit energetically. They are often drawn to someone like Don who is still alive but has been on drugs, alcohol, or other abusive substances. Don and others like him who are heavily "under the influence" are not in full command. Their energy field becomes vulnerable to lost beings. Adepts who are clairvoyant and tuned into this visual frequency can track the movement of the lost beings as they seek refuge.

I had never been able to relate to this information, but suddenly I thought of the megadoses of narcotics Don had ingested. He was obviously not the captain of his ship right now. Once again, my curiosity took the lead. While Don was sleeping, I called an energy worker who was experienced with this type of thing, and she gave me a verbal energetic clearing. When she told me it was a simple process, I imagined it to be in the same category as the "boost" I had administered to Gloria, my hospice patient.

When Don woke up and continued cackling variations of the weird sound "Koo-kah, koo-kah," I followed my friend's advice and commanded, "Whoever or whatever you are inhabiting Don's body, please leave now." I stated my desire to discontinue any relationship with this body as long as it was not being controlled by Don. I told the lost being to go back to wherever it came from. As I emphatically made this command, Don's face froze and he instantly stopped all vocalization. His bulging eyes closed abruptly and his head fell back onto the pillow.

A few hours later, in the middle of the night, I was in a chair next to Don's bed. As I watched his eyes open, I shifted from the chair to the bed, tucking my legs underneath me. When I leaned in toward his face, it was clear that his eyes had a different quality. What was it? I knew that quality ... he was there, he was conscious of himself, of the room, of me. It had been thirteen days since I had experienced that connection with him.

With my face six inches from his, I spoke softly. "Don, do you know who I am? Do you know I am your wife?" He nodded "Yes."

"Are you in pain?" He shook his head "No."

"Are you depressed?" Again, he nodded "Yes."

Then my last question ... "Do you know I love you?"

With his deep brown eyes locked with mine, there was a slow, deliberate nod. "Yes."

From this turning point, my job became navigating that connection with very little verbal communication. Although I craved to talk out loud to Don, encouraging him to respond, I became an observer, tuning in to all the subtleties in his world.

To assist Don with his neurology and spinal column, I hired a therapist, Deidra, who was trained in the Feldenkrais method. This therapy was developed by Dr. Moshe Feldenkrais as a means to re-engage the nervous system in the kind of learning that unfolds in infants. It was necessary to slip Deidra in under the hospital radar, using the term "neuromuscular re-education" with which the administration was familiar. She was able to impact Don's spinal column and brain by gently moving his arms, legs, hands, and feet.

The night after their session, I woke up to find Don diligently attempting to replicate the flowing movements she had orchestrated for him. I was fully present, encouraging him in the silence. He lifted a leg and lowered it, and then he raised and lowered his eyebrows as if to say, "Well done, Corf." Then he lifted his arm, swinging it slowly to his brow and back. Success again! He seemed to be in a process of "discovery"— maybe he was discerning what it would take to bring his body back online.

Most of the hospice staff members were kind and diligent, and they were eager to make Don comfortable. However, they were unfamiliar with the more subtle world of communication and recovery. During the day, the hospice physician stopped in to review and chart Don's progress. She spoke in a loud, demanding voice, as if by doing so there would be a greater chance of Don understanding her "orders." She would issue commands and then make notes regarding whether and how he responded.

"Mr. Corfman, move your fingers for me," she ordered. I was surprised to see Don's eyes lowered in humiliation. His fingers and hands appeared paralyzed. The night before, I had quietly watched him study the movement of his hands like a child discovering his fingers and toes for the first time. With great deliberation, he had moved each finger successfully. Now it was as if, by not "performing" to the doctor's standards, Don felt like a failure. It wasn't until later that I found out from a speech pathologist that moving his fingers voluntarily required the use of a different part of the brain than initiating movement based on a demand.

After testing his motor skills, Don began experimenting with his voice. My sister Robbie was staying with him while I took a break one evening. He made some distressing noises and Robbie jumped up and asked him, "Don, do you need help?" He said, "Help! Help! Help!" Robbie asked, "How?" and he repeated, "How? How? How?" She asked if he was in pain. He said, "No, No, No." Did he want water? "Yes, Yes, Yes."

When the nurse brought him water, she asked him, "Do you want water, sir?" Forever the gentleman—even after coming out of a coma—he replied, "Yes, please."

Wanting to make sure Don didn't need additional "help," Robbie had the nurse check Don to make sure he was dry. With all the basic needs covered, it seemed that Don's repeating of her words was a way he could re-learn to speak complete sentences. Along with this voice activation, he continued raising his arms up and holding them on top of his head as the Feldenkrais practitioner had done with him.

While sitting with Don, it was my younger sister, Pattie, who first noticed his sense of humor resurfacing. When she clumsily knocked the bed rail with the book she was reading to him, she said to Don, who had been resting with his eyes closed, "Oops, I know I'm supposed to be quiet." He gave her a big grin.

The book was one of mine, about the evolution of consciousness. As she read some of it aloud to him, his eyes grew heavy and sleepy. Pattie said, "Don, this book is pretty dense and boring. It makes me sleepy, too." Again, a big grin flashed across his face. It had always been a joke between Don and me that, while I read my philosophical favorites before falling asleep at night, he would lie beside me reading something much more fun and steamy, like a trashy novel.

Under Pattie's watch, Don again was moving his legs and arms a lot. He even tried to sit up on his own. "Crap," he said when he wasn't successful. Then he made a motion like touching his nose or even scratching it. With the successful gestures, he nodded "Yes" to himself. Unsure of what was going on, Pattie asked, "Do you need something, Don?" Again he laughed. As if reading his mind, she said, "All kinds of things, right?" He nodded.

During this time, Don's basketball and golfing buddies streamed in to be with him. It was uncomfortable for them to see such drastic and sudden changes in his health, and initially, they would get choked up. For these guys in their fifties and sixties, Don was a glaring mirror for their own fragility and mortality. But eventually, in spite of this, they appealed to Don's outlandish sense of humor, and the visits were filled with joviality.

Don would smile and do his best to respond, but after their visits, he was often exhausted. In his condition, it took an enormous amount of energy to function. Although he never showed it to his visitors, I sensed that the visits were sometimes frustrating to him because his limited communication skills became accentuated. I began guiding the amount of time devoted to others so he would have the time he needed for his organs and his body to recover.

Don's awareness continued to increase, and we consistently tuned in to his choices. Even in hospice, it was important to avoid becoming robotic in what was offered to us. One night, the nurse came in and asked him if he was in pain. Don said, "No." A short time later, she approached me and wanted to give Don a sedative so he could get his "nights back" and resume a normal sleep schedule. When I explained to Don what the nurse suggested, Don emphatically shook his head "No." Two hours later, another nurse named Chris came in to give Don Tylenol when he heard him moaning.

"Let's ask Don first what he needs," I said. When Chris held up the Tylenol, Don said, "No." Then I asked Don, "Are you in pain?" He shook his head "No."

Chris admitted to me that he was never sure if Don was cognizant of what he was being asked. I let Chris know. "Absolutely, he knows and is aware of what you are saying. Just ask him and he will let you know what he wants."

"I can see that now," Chris replied.

With all of this progress, I was getting more and more hopeful of moving Don out of hospice, but it was suggested we order Don a new, extra-long mattress, because he was so tall that his feet hung over the end of the bed. The hospice doctors reminded me that patients often have a huge improvement in their condition before taking a turn for the worse. I was fully aware of this, but I felt that Don's situation could be the exception. Then I agreed that the longer bed was a good idea. That evening, as Robbie laid in the bed next to Don's, ready to go to sleep, Don said, loud and clear: "Terrie?!"

It was the first time he had uttered my name since that night in ICU when I kissed him goodbye—and it would be the last.

Robbie went to him and said, "Don, Terrie went home to get some sleep. Will you miss her?"

He said, "Yes."

The rest of the night, Don was making sounds and didn't sleep. The sounds were not those associated with pain. Several times, he said, "Oh boy, oh boy." He took short, quick breaths as his stomach went up and down, and Robbie thought he was laughing. Then she realized he wasn't laughing. He was crying without tears.

When I arrived early the next morning, I sat beside Don. He looked into my eyes and he took my hand in his. He raised my hand to his mouth and pretended to gnaw on my knuckles. When I started laughing, he bit a little harder and gave me a playful look. For the first time since the coma, my humorous, intimate connection with him was back. I squeezed his hand and whispered, "Don, would you like me to run energy on your back?" He nodded.

With my palms on the back of his torso, I felt a soft throbbing under my hands. Then the vibration expanded and enveloped both of us. There was an overriding sense of lightness and joy. For a moment, I felt like we didn't have physical bodies and we were dangling in a space beyond the room. I felt no need for anything in this infinite spaciousness. But then a music therapist named Wyatt appeared at the doorway with his guitar. As he started playing "Blowing in the Wind," Don's eyes lit up and a big smile spread across his face. I listened to the words ..." *How many seas must a white dove sail before she sleeps in the sand? ... The answer is blowin' in the wind.*"

Hearing the music and seeing the beauty and serenity on Don's face was too much. In spite of what Balbir had told me about keeping my emotions at bay, I just let the tears stream down my cheeks, unchecked. They were a river collected from twenty days of bridled emotion. I felt gut-wrenching love, and it encompassed all. My last thought, while gazing at Don as the song ended, was, "He is such a good-looking man ..."

I thanked Wyatt for playing. After he left, Don's beautiful gaze became a sterile stare at the ceiling. And then came the final turning point. A gray pallor drifted over his face like a cloud slowly moving past the sun. His eyes became glassy. I could feel terror in the pit of my stomach. "No!" my mind screamed, "I won't let it happen again."

Kathryn, a hospice nurse who was a dear friend of mine, had been assigned to Don that morning. Knowing I could trust her, I raced to find her and frantically asked, "Kathryn, what is happening?" Calmly, she held my hand and said, "Terrie, you know. He just entered the active phase of dying."

From my experience with patients, I knew all too well that what she said was true. But this time, it was my husband, not a hospice patient.

She said, "Terrie, I will make him as comfortable as possible." My heart sank, and for a moment I wanted to forget how many times I had told Don that I would support whatever choice he made. I wanted to cling, clutch, and hold onto him for dear life. This was devastating, after five days of increased hope.

Kathryn went to Don's side to straighten his pillow, and as she barely jostled his head on the pillow, he screamed in agony. The pain contorted his face. All false hope vanished in that moment, and I surrendered.

I spent the next twenty-four hours vigilant at Don's side. We put off any feeding and bathing until he could be free from pain.

Later that afternoon, while Don was sleeping, I reviewed the signs of the dying process with Kathryn. By evening, Don's eyes were half closed, even when he was awake. He became less and less alert. We continued giving him a sedative and pain medication to keep him free of discomfort. At bedtime, my sister and I slid, side by side, into the single bed next to Don's. We cuddled and she held me while I drifted off to sleep, exhausted.

The next morning was September 23, the day that would be imprinted forever on Don's death certificate. I spent the day in a vigil of watching and waiting—the day of allowance. The doctor had told me Don might survive another five days because he hadn't lost much weight and wasn't wasting away. And like birth, death is organic, beyond prediction.

That evening, upon returning from Sultan's, where my sister and I downed a soothing bowl of lentil soup, Robbie and I were prepared to put on our pajamas and get some sleep before facing the week ahead of us. The waiting could be so draining. By now, relatives and friends were gone. Everyone had come by to pay their respects and say their good-byes, so it was just my sister and me.

When we walked in, Don made a sound. His head turned slightly toward me, like an acknowledgment that he knew we had returned. Within five minutes, his breathing became congested and he started the familiar "death rattle." We pulled up two chairs. I took hold of Don's hand with my left hand, and held Robbie's hand with my right. Inhale, exhale. Inhale, exhale. We all three breathed in unison.

Once again, it felt peaceful and other-worldly, as if somehow we were not in the room, but floating in unison in some spacious light. Don inhaled, and this time, I held my breath, waiting … within a few seconds he exhaled. Again, a long, labored inhale … holding my breath again, I waited for Don's cue—but this time, it never came. I looked at Robbie and a mixture of jubilation and sadness came over both of us.

We sat together with Don for the next half hour in silence, feeling peace, love, and gratitude for everything he had been for us and everything we had shared with him. When the nurse stopped in, I said, "I think he just took his last breath."

It was then she did all the "checking" that they do, and some moments of minor chaos ensued. But the divine passing had already been orchestrated. We had wanted to postpone the medical agenda so as not to disturb anything connected to his passing.

That night, with Robbie lying on Don's side of the bed and me lying on my side, I was so grateful her arms were there to hold me as Don's had for the past seven years. It occurred to me how commonplace it had seemed to crawl into bed every night with Don. I had taken it for granted.

The next morning was filled with the profound and the mundane.

The first thing I did was email Balbir. I let him know Don had passed peacefully at 7:15 p.m. the night before and that Robbie and I were with him. Immediately, I received an email response.

"Dearest Terrie,

Last night, Treva and I were taking a short hike with our friends in the Rockies. We were huffing and puffing in the pure, thin air above 10,000 feet, when I saw Don, you, and Robbie. For a split second, I was there with you and felt Don was saying goodbye. Simultaneously, Don was here on the top of the mountain with me. For me, it was a divine experience. Seeing Don was as real as if he was standing in front of me. So as I opened your email, I knew what your message would be."

Robbie was in the kitchen as I was reading the email out loud. When I got to the sentence, "Don was here with me" there was a clap of thunder that shook the condo. There was no lightening, no clouds, no rain, and no other ensuing thunder. Then the cremation representative handling my affairs knocked on my front door. When I opened it, he looked incredulous and said, "Wow, did you hear that thunder?"

As if someone had told us to "chop wood, carry water" after a profound spiritual experience, Robbie and I went to Nordstrom and we stood at the cosmetic counter buying new make-up. The clerk was kind and helpful. It was an indelible moment, etched in time. I remember every detail. Along with the make-up, I found a sleeveless blue dress to wear to Don's memorial service. Later, these final moments were crafted, as Robbie had promised, into a poem. She captured the experience for me with the beauty of the words on the following pages:

The Last Time I Saw You
by Robbie Curry

I

The last time I saw you
your naked feet were jammed
against the footboard—
you were too tall—
your body slipping away
from the pillow,
the pain, the pain
every time a nurse
shifted you to fit.

We had returned from dinner.
Your eyes surprised us, your breathing—

you were leaving when you could have stayed.

We hitched a ride with you to the border,
transported by each breath we breathed
in unison.

You noticed and seemed to pick up speed—

somehow it wasn't terrifying.

Swiftly you crossed over.

You left us, at the end
of an ancient road, empty
but for dust kicked up
by a gale-force wind that blew
through us, our eyes stinging,
straining to see.

When we returned, we gazed
at a vacant stranger, strangely
satisfied, as if we had cheered
you on from the backseat.

II

You would have accomplished it
without us, but you waited,
always the gentleman.

After they took your body away,
and we went back to the house, and
I took your side of the bed,
and we held each other, the night wept.

The next day she made arrangements
at St. Mary's. We drove to Nordstrom.
She bought new blush and a blue dress,
sleeveless in winter.

CHAPTER 7

Grief, Birth, and Finally a Return Homeward

I have always been a fan of celebrating one's life in a gathering with friends and family. I am not for burying or cremating someone and acting as if there is nothing to acknowledge and no fanfare to be had. Maybe it comes from the first funeral I attended as a third-grader. It was my grandfather who had died. I had never known him. He was in a VA Hospital for twenty years, declared legally insane due to injuries from nerve gas used in WWI. He was awarded the Purple Heart. His body was brought to our hometown, and there was an open-casket Catholic rosary that the entire brood attended.

All of my first and second cousins, uncles and aunts from my big, Catholic family were there for the death of the patriarch. There is still a photograph etched in my memory of how he looked in the coffin. Some of my cousins, I knew well. Others, I had never met before. We gathered at the home of my grandmother for a day-long celebration. Her house was like a second home for my siblings and me.

My memory of grandfather's passing is still one of laughter, play, and camaraderie. The highlight was riding with ten of my cousins crammed, standing up, onto the seats of a 1963 Volkswagen Beetle. Ten heads were popped up through the sun roof as my uncle turned corners like a race-car driver while we screamed in glee. From a child's perspective, I remember it as one of the best days of my life. Ever since, funerals have filled me with the same sense of joyful connection.

At Don's gathering, there was a different sense of connectivity. The people who assembled reflected the time in our lives. There were no religious ties or blood-lines as a bonding agent. Blended families were a common denominator—his former wife showed up with her estranged daughter, to whom Don had actually become close. Friends came from his first marriage, as well as "the basketball network" or the fraternity of college athletes who were the springboard for his IT career. Familiar faces included Jon and Cassie, the couple who had sparked our entire journey; my extended family; the neighborhood dog-walkers; and happily, the sixteen Faith Academy basketball players.

I coaxed a Catholic priest to perform the service in a church that Don and I were fond of but had never attended. The historic St. Mary's Cathedral was half a block from our condo, and we passed it daily on our bike rides. We awaited each spring for the return of Horatio, the falcon who came annually to nest in the church steeple. He mated and produced offspring that we joyfully watched take their first flights. And it was fun seeing young newlyweds emerge from the big, wooden doors with smiles for a promising future together.

Built in 1885, then re-built and preserved after the great Chicago fire, St. Mary's was a beautiful structure with stained-glass windows. I'm pretty sure the Catholic priest was drunk at our funeral ceremony, but I was grateful he allowed us into his sanctuary. He had reminded me that allowing this memorial service in the Cathedral for a "non-Catholic" was a generous act on his part (although the fact that I had been baptized a Catholic at birth was like having a green card).

The highlight of the service for everyone was hearing "Don's boys" as they each stepped up to the podium to casually and authentically describe the Don they had come to know.

D.J. spoke first. "When Mr. C came to our school, I thought he was another old, stupid white guy telling me what to do. But he was different. He really taught me stuff, and he cared. He was so funny."

Willie, who pulled up the rear, finished with, "Coach C was like a grandfather to me. I could trust him. And I'm bad at math but he was a genius and showed me math problems can be easy. I will miss him."

I knew if Don was watching this celebration from a non-physical place, he would be smiling, just like he did on the basketball court. And maybe he was leaping into the air for a slam dunk.

Before I was able to catch my breath, after celebrating Don's life with those close to me, more tragedy unfolded. It added to the intensity I was experiencing with Don's absence. Within two weeks, I was called away from Chicago to be with my father, who had entered hospice as he went through the final stages of cancer.

With his death a month after Don's, I had an opportunity to experience the effect on the psyche of multiple and almost simultaneous deaths. In hospice, I had often wondered how a mother bears the loss of more than one child. Like Agnes, who had lost five of her six children to a genetic disease. Or Maria, who lost her only two children in a tragic accident. No one ever wants to think of these things. It's something to be lived through, not thought about. The shock to the system is numbing. Otherwise, it might be unbearable.

For me, the shock culminated in a moment when I was driving by myself from the hospital to my father's house, a route I knew well. All of a sudden, I felt lost. I pulled off to the side of the road, crawled into the back seat, curled up, and lay there, trembling, unable to think or decide where I was going or what I should do next. In that moment, my cell phone rang. It was my daughter, checking up on me. Like a guardian angel, she offered to come and assist me.

It was obvious that I was far more vulnerable than any of my four siblings. I had always thought I would be the stronghold for them in my father's death. I had both financial and legal expertise in estate matters, as well as the emotional fortitude for end-of life-issues. In their eyes, I was the queen of death and dying. Needless to say, I failed as their pillar.

The paradox of being with my husband and father, one after the other, in their final hours, is that my father was completely verbal, and yet he appeared confused because of his dementia. Don had been very clear-headed, and yet he could barely speak.

There was something a bit strange underlying my communication with my father. He had been CFO of a major corporation, mentoring and guiding me in my financial career. He was described as a "straight shooter" by those who deeply respected his candor and integrity.

Now as I held his hand, I observed what I called the "unwinding of the left brain." His voice was rational and without any trace of emotion as he told me how scary it was for him that his ideas weren't making sense anymore. He couldn't take his ideas to a point of origin. "How can I ever trust myself again?" he asked.

That evening at his bedside, I whispered to my sister while he was sleeping, "Dad is dying exactly how he lived. The whole process is a very rational one for him." With that comment barely out of my mouth, he opened his eyes, sat straight up, and pointed his finger at me. "You are exactly right," he said.

Intermittently, he would see a being he described as "Michael" on the ceiling of the room. He asked me if I could see him. I said, "No, Dad, but I believe you can see him." Then I asked, "What is he saying?"

My dad replied, "He says just keep doing my work." Once again, I was seeing a glimpse of receptivity from a very linear mind.

Amidst all this coming to terms with the finality of death, I had almost forgotten about the magic of birth. In November, like a cool breeze that eases the heat on a blistering summer day, my first grandchild was born in Kansas City. He was a big, healthy baby, the son of his six-foot-four-inch father who wanted him to be a basketball player and an all-around athlete. Maybe he would be a "leaper" like Don. I smiled at the thought. It felt soothing to be a part of his new life: to hold him, to rock him, to sing to him. It was healing for me to be with him and watch the ever-changing stages of a newborn. His wide-eyed fascination with sounds, shapes, color, and movement added vibrancy to my life. But I knew, as the New Year approached, that I must return to Chicago.

It was Saturday night, January 21, 2012 when I arrived at Midway Airport. It was sobering when we landed to see myself turn on my cell phone to text Don, only to realize he would not be there to taxi me home. As I stepped outside, the snow and ice had begun to crystallize, and it jolted me into winter. The numbing shock of September events began to subside.

When I walked into our condo, my heart melted into the memories. While grocery shopping, I found myself lingering in the produce section to get a whiff of fresh basil. I purposefully crumbled fresh rosemary in my hand to intoxicate me. In our garden, in the dead of winter, I could swear I smelled cilantro. And there was a painful absence of the aromas which had formerly filled the kitchen—chestnut soup, Moroccan lamb stew, and laksa. All those favorite recipes of Don's which I had never written down.

I found support and kindness everywhere, sometimes in the most unlikely places. One night as I was approaching my condo after visiting a friend, I noticed Beatrice and Wally, two of Don's favorite dogs, walking toward me. They were pulling their owner, who was a faceless figure in the dark. I heard her say, "How are you doing?" I had never met this woman, but I recognized her. She was one of the dog walkers, a fraternity all its own—a fraternity where owners, first and foremost, knew all the mutts and pedigrees by name, and only as a secondary politeness they came to know the names of one another.

I was surprised that this woman I didn't even know would show concern. "I'm doing okay. Thank you," I said.

"Your husband was one of the kindest men I have ever met," she said with such sincerity, I believed her. Then, due to the bitter cold, we said a hurried good night. As I closed the door to my condo, I remembered what Dannion Brinkley, author of "Saved by the Light," had described as paramount in his two near-death experiences: He had been told that what truly matters when you cross over are the acts of kindness you have shared.

Hazmek and Charles, our ninety-something neighbors, became a lifeline. Hazmek had been born in the big house on Mohawk Street where her father had a storefront selling tamales. Charles was from Georgia. He was still the quintessential gentleman with a Southern drawl. They had lived out their careers successfully in music theatre and opera. Charles had also been a copyist, he had one client left who would pay for manual and handwritten, non-digitalized scores. I would spend evenings listening to them singing arias on old recordings while Hazmek served me hot bowls of homemade soup.

Around 10 p.m. one night, when I saw a suspicious character loitering on the street as I parked my car, I called them. I let Charles know it was just a heads-up that I was parking my car in the alley and I would be walking the half block to my condo. I would call again if I ran into any trouble. Charles insisted he meet me at my front door to make sure I got in okay. When I resisted, he became so insistent that I realized this was chivalry at its finest, and I'd better acquiesce. It reminded me of Don. It was something he would do if he had lived to ninety.

Finally, spring arrived, and the flowers in our garden bloomed—the tiger lilies, daffodils, lilies of the valley. The yellow and white tulips opened, but I was waiting for the "bed of red." As I biked through Lincoln Park, I noticed the red tulips flourishing all around Old Town—yet the one clump Don had affectionately planted for me three years earlier remained slumped over and brown. They were the only flowers in our garden that didn't blossom in the spring of 2012. "Maybe they are just sad like me," I thought.

When the numbness had subsided that January, I had also started looking at my emotions through a lens. First, I became aware that grief was a feeling that I believed kept me "connected" to Don. Something in me knew that, as the grief eased, there would be a simultaneous lessening in my visceral tie to him. Since he hadn't had a long illness and I hadn't had any preparation for his health crisis, coming to grips with his death had felt like an abrupt cliff rather than a gentle slope. I was grateful now to be able to choose my own pace. There was a sense of freedom with that choice.

The second emotion I observed was guilt. I found that the greatest letting go was in not making myself "wrong" for what I did or didn't do, or what I was or wasn't aware of. In the beginning, it was difficult for me to accept that, under my loving watch, I had still been so out of touch with the serious nature of Don's condition. However, after his death, I started experiencing Don's presence in so many ways that I began to feel reassured that, in fact, I had been an invaluable companion in those final days.

Through hospice, I had become familiar with the many ways families and friends receive communication with someone after they die. Such communication is actually quite common, but not everyone is willing to talk about it. In one of her books, Kubler-Ross mentions several of the common methods of contact occurring with deceased patients: apparitions, nature, dreams, touch, and synchronicity. Observing Kubler-Ross's willingness to include all kinds of paranormal experiences in her observation as a scientist was very helpful to me. It allowed me to circumvent my rational mind in order to perceive the possibilities beyond death.

Of all the methods, an apparition—actually seeing the person in full body form—is the rarest. In one situation, a deceased patient named Mrs. Schwartz appeared to Kubler-Ross while on an elevator. She came to give Kubler-Ross a message to continue her work with the dying and confirmed for Kubler-Ross that death isn't what we think it is. Don's appearance to Balbir after his death was uplifting for me. It let me know that the perception of death as a prelude to something greater was not only possible, but probable.

Kubler-Ross discovered dreams were the most common method of contact from the deceased. I received much comfort and reassurance through dreams. The first dream when Don showed up, we were sitting beside each other having an intimate conversation. I felt half awake and half asleep. He and I were sharing how much we meant to each other, and the gratitude we felt for each other. As he was talking to me, a memory slipped into my mind, and I thought, "Oh, no, but he's dead." The moment that thought came in, Don looked me in the eye and said, "Terrie, I do not exist where your memory is. I am not your memory of me." With that, I came fully awake, and his presence was gone. It felt as if I had been physically with him.

I found that the more open I was and the less I tried to make sense of it all, the greater understanding and sense of peace I received from his communication.

One day, I met my friend Michelle for lunch. She was very clairvoyant. Her capacity often frightened her, as it does some people who are tuned into this gift. She walked in quite joyfully and we had a nice lunch. At the end she said, "Oh, I almost forgot to tell you. Don visited me in my meditation this morning and he told me to tell you he is really happy. He said to tell you not to be sad, that you still need to be here. And he said, 'Tell Terrie it's like I'm on a great vacation.'"

I believed Michelle, because she didn't seem attached at all to the message nor to the fact Don had chosen her as the messenger. Don had also thanked her for being there for me and for being willing to deliver his message to me.

In my year of exploration, I happened to meet a young man named Clark who had experienced multiple near-death experiences at the age of thirteen. He had been in a car accident and had lost his short-term memory. Over a five-year period, he was shown, by non-physical guides, how to heal his brain and memory. In the process, he had learned a great deal about the movement of energy and what happens with energy at the moment of death.

I told him I would like to experience what Don went through as he died, because at the time I had felt expansion and joy, and now I could only remember those last moments with grief. I had read how Steven Levine, a famous hospice advocate, had requested to experience this with one of his patients. He was given an experience in simultaneous time just before his friend died.

Clark agreed to guide me energetically through a process of those last moments. We started a meditation. He described how the energy was at the feet, and how it moved up from the feet to the solar plexus, to the heart, then to the crown. I was having difficulty feeling the energy in my body as Clark was talking me through it. Oddly enough, everything he described was being expressed outside on my patio. The wind began a powerful swirling movement similar to the vortex Clark was describing inside the body. This was the power of the energy as the spirit leaves the body.

Suddenly, the wind on the patio became so strong it lifted the glass table top where Don had served so many guests. Then the tabletop crashed on the concrete and shattered into a thousand pieces. The pile of glass was a powerful image for me. It reminded me that, while our structure here is temporary, our energy is infinite. A calm settled over me after the experience was over. Metaphor had once again winked at me, unexpectedly.

CHAPTER 8

Healing, Humor, and Brighter Horizons

In June of 2012, an event took place that catapulted me out of Chicago sooner than I had expected. Megan came with the baby for a week-long visit. We strolled baby Trystan through the streets of Old Town to get our morning lattes and enjoyed sunny days at the Farmers' Market and Lincoln Park Zoo. After encouraging her to let me babysit while she took some time for herself, she headed out one late afternoon to get a massage.

Around 7 p.m., Trystan and I were upstairs playing when the doorbell rang. I knew it was Megan—she had left without a key. As I put the baby on my hip and headed downstairs, I said, smiling, "Trystan, Mommy's home."

Just then, I heard Megan's blood-curdling cry. She started screaming, "I will fucking kill you!"

Pause. "He's got a gun!"

As I reached the door seconds later, my hand froze on the door knob. Her message had been loud and clear: *There's an armed man outside your door. Keep my baby safe.*

A quick mental picture of my choices flashed through my mind. I saw myself open the door just enough to pull her in. I stopped the thought of what might happen if I didn't open the door. The mind rehearsal played out, and Megan stumbled in hysterically as we slammed the door behind her. Her head was badly beaten, but she hadn't been shot. When she had felt the assailant tap her on the shoulder and had seen a silver gun held to her chest, she had risen in fury like a mama bear protecting her cub. She knew she had to be massively bigger and stronger than the gunman who wanted to force his way in.

As she fought off her attacker, people started appearing on the street, potential witnesses. He was distracted by their intrusion. He grabbed Megan's cell phone, which she had dropped in the scuffle, and then casually sauntered away. It was in that moment that I had opened the door.

After the incident, I knew in a primal way what mothers and grandmothers lived with on the South Side of Chicago. They felt terror, day in and day out, knowing that their children and grandchildren might die in a random act of violence. Because of this new trauma, I chose to put my home on the market—"For Sale By Owner"—and leave my life in Chicago.

I could feel the pull of brighter horizons. Although a condo glut gripped the city and prices were depressed, once again the Universe had my back. A British couple, disappointed after looking at thirty properties with their realtor, strayed from their normal routine one day and decided to walk down Eugenie Street instead. They fell in love with my place at first sight. We made a deal, and within three weeks, I was headed to Colorado for a Rocky Mountain high.

After twenty years in Chicago, even with family in Denver, the Wild West gave me culture shock. These were Home-on-the-(Front) Range extreme-sports addicts stoned on brownies. And if I thought I could remain a city slicker, those hopes were dashed the moment the lady in the cowboy hat and spurs greeted me at the information booth in the Denver International Airport.

But soon, the magic of the mountains became a source of inspiration, and I began writing. Little by little, Colorado's geographic splendor seeped into my bones and I felt beauty all around me. Writing became like breathing as I described the things I loved: the tenacity and innocence of the children on the South Side of Chicago and the brilliance imbued in the children I knew diagnosed with autism. As the family octogenarians began leaving us, one by one, I commemorated them by writing about their traits so they would be humorously remembered.

I discovered that emotion can be a powerful outlet for creation. To my surprise, creativity was the catalyst that moved me into a joyful life. After losing a spouse, there can be a tendency to replace your lost joy with someone new. It surprised me that it was writing that shifted my emotional energy into action, expansion, and possibility.

The discovery that humor is cathartic was not new. Yet to see it come alive in me as I moved through my own grief was fascinating. I became curious and watched what made other people laugh, and what made me laugh: timing, or self-deprecation, or vulnerability. Humor acknowledged my darkest moments, yet lightened their burden.

While watching a movie in which Diane Keaton portrayed and embellished a grief-stricken widow, I saw myself in metaphor. She was a singer at a night club, crying in the middle of every song. As she wiped her face with Kleenex, her elongated sadness became comical. The scene struck a chord. I couldn't get through a gourmet meal without tearing up, just remembering what a fantastic cook Don had been. Laughter effortlessly transmuted my tragedy into a comedy. Of course, Don himself continued interjecting humor in my life. When I asked him what title I should give this book, the answer that came was *Don, But Not Forgotten.*

In addition to paying attention to my emotions and the messages and assistance from Don, I paid attention to the impact touch and bodywork could have on my health and well-being.

It began during a yoga therapy session. As I moved my leg, I heard the words, "You will find God in your body." To tell you the truth, that is the last rock I would have looked under. Transcending the body had been embedded in all of my spiritual practices.

After that, I started getting regular massages, because it made me feel better and reduced the stress in my life. I experimented with BARS, Feldenkrais, and craniosacral therapy. As I began to feel the more subtle vibrations and less dense forms of touch, my body became a conduit accessing the deeper, hidden layers of my being.

Just as science now has the technology to photograph the infinite nature of our DNA, and the Hubble spacecraft boasts images of galaxies beyond our own, I began to perceive the body as an instrument from which I might tap into this full spectrum. My body, brain, spine, and nervous system were like probes receiving and transmitting information in the form of profound awarenesses regarding all kinds of things. The more I worked with universal energy, the more I found that I didn't know "how" it worked just "that" it worked.

Once during a Feldenkrais session, as the practitioner reminded me that movement is the journey and not the destination, I could feel Don's energetic body embedded in my own. When my arm moved, his moved, and when my leg moved, his leg moved. Soon, we were moving in unison in a fluid dance of wonder, as if we were integral parts of some vaster embodiment.

BARS, an energy process, which is run on thirty-two points on the head, was powerful help in releasing the memories locked into my cells from the trauma. The process began deleting negative programs in my brain like a computer deletes outdated files. By receiving this brain and bodywork weekly during the year after Don died, I felt greater ease.

As I experienced healing, I was still bothered by the question: Why do we feel grief at all? The root of this question stemmed from having read the book, *Mutant Message Down Under* by Marlo Morgan, many years before. Morgan spins a tale of a mysterious walkabout with an aboriginal tribe who call themselves the Real People. They live a nomadic life in the most desolate part of the desert in the Australian outback—yet they live a magical life of wholeness, oneness, and telepathy. They don't experience sadness and grief, because they do not feel separation or judgment. Death to them is just another possibility to be celebrated. They lovingly describe the white man as a Mutant who is mutating his way into Oneness. I realized that so many of my experiences were giving me glimpses of Oneness. I wanted to continue to be guided into that state of being.

Financial, Legal, and Medical Underpinnings

Some say we are human beings having a spiritual experience, and others say we are spiritual beings having a human experience. No matter which way you see it, we don't skip any part of the journey. Rather than letting our human affairs run amok, we learn to deal with what is, not what we think could or should be.

Sometimes we think of financial, legal, and medical issues as a nightmare of unnecessary complexity. While this may be true, the key is knowing the ins and outs of how we can make it all work for us. We can and we must learn to pay attention to these "matters"—literally, those things that "deal with matter." I believe that in doing so, we are actually contributing to our life and to the lives of those around us.

The first few days Don was in the hospice wing at St. Germain, something unimaginable occurred. The ward was quiet, with the appearance of few visitors. Don ended up in a private room that had a cozy feel to it, so I made myself at home, leaving my things strewn on the chair. My purse was left unzipped for my easy access. It contained Don's billfold which I had secured when he was admitted to the emergency room.

One evening as I glanced at it, I had a funny feeling inside. I felt an urge to open Don's billfold. Uneasiness gnawed at me when I noticed his debit and credit cards were missing. I was baffled, because I had been in the room the whole time except for quick trips to the restroom down the hallway. To my alarm, when I checked online, I found a string of unauthorized debits to Walmart, Best Buy, and Jewel Foods etc. ringing up over $1,000 in charges.

The next morning, I notified Gaston, a young, gregarious personal banker with whom I had bonded. For cheerfully handling all of our banking needs, I had occasionally bestowed upon him homemade, chocolate chip cookies. With compassionate concern, Gaston calmed me and then instructed me to come in tomorrow, if possible, with a copy of the Power of Attorney form showing me as agent. In the meantime, he would put a stop on debits to Don's checking and credit card accounts. His voice was filled with caring and warmth as he said, "Don't worry, Ms. Curry. We will take care of you."

The hospice was upset and apologetic for this breach of trust I had to endure in such a vulnerable time. Yet it was the bank that had the expertise to handle and cover the fraudulent act.

As a financial analyst with estate planning expertise, I had experienced firsthand the convenience of knowing your banker. Additionally, I had come to know that there was a pragmatic underpinning to death and dying. I worked with a lawyer who had many elderly clients. I had witnessed many stories that left a vivid impression on me. The main message was this: With a little advance attention to detail, you can spare your loved ones much stress when you die.

This awareness helped to ease the challenges I faced as Don's health declined in the hospital, as well as during the aftermath once he had passed. Attending to a loved one in the hospital is already stressful; the steps that I outline here can help make life a little easier for everyone involved. In the appendix of the book, you will also find an abbreviated checklist to help you remember the tips I give you. Knowledge is power, and when you have it on your side, you can be the best advocate for those who matter most to you.

Before Don went in for his ablation procedure, I had a check-list of medical details to cover, mostly pertaining to being Don's advocate. I wanted to be able to access his information in case he wasn't in a position to do so himself.

Don had HMO insurance. We called the provider to determine what we needed so that I would be authorized to get any and all medical information by telephone. We filled out the paperwork, sent it in, and did a dry run. When I called, however, they wouldn't give me information. We repeated the procedure until I was able to call and easily receive information by phone.

Another important aspect of managing your insurance is understanding your healthcare network. We had to think ahead on this one, because the surgeon Don had chosen was out of network, which required special permission from the insurance company. For any follow-up work that was also out of network, we would have to call Don's primary physician and get the okay. This piece of information proved to be invaluable during Don's health crisis as we had to obtain more procedures out of network. It was helpful to have this process already streamlined when it was difficult to think about necessary details. Because we understood these guidelines ahead of time, I avoided conflict and debate over the medical costs billed thereafter.

Like many couples, Don and I had always had our own bank accounts. Although we separated our finances, we wanted to be sure we both had access in case anything should happen, so we put our names on each other's accounts as POD, "Payable on Death." That meant the money was then immediately available to either of us in the event of spousal death without having to probate it. We also went over all of our brokerage and retirement accounts and made sure they were titled properly in joint tenancy or we were named as beneficiaries on the relevant beneficiary forms. By doing this, all assets could easily be liquidated upon death, rather than having to wait for up to nine months for their release in probate of the estate.

I recommend making a list of any accounts you have—insurance policies, bank and brokerage accounts, home-ownership documents, etc.—that might need to be accessed in the event of your death or the death of your partner.. Keeping them all together in a lockbox (either at home or at a bank) is helpful, because of the chaos that seems to surround death. Don had been meticulous in his detail and order of things, and this was a blessing for me. Attention to detail might seem like a pain in the neck, but it is a form of caring for those you leave behind.

From a legal standpoint, three documents are important to have in place: Power of Attorney for Healthcare, a Will, and Power of Attorney for Property.

In the most general sense, these documents will grant you the ability to make decisions and act on behalf of your loved one. They also allow your loved one to clearly state how they wish their affairs to be handled in the event they are incapacitated or deceased.

Paperwork for POAs can be acquired from any hospice organization, or you can opt for a lawyer to guide you through the process. Knowing the importance of having a Power of Attorney for Healthcare in place, Don and I had obtained Illinois's statutory form from a local hospice. I had learned that doctors and hospitals are familiar with this statutory form and recognize its legal authority without having to read the fine print. This form allowed Don to specify in writing whom he trusted to make decisions regarding his health.

While Don was in a coma, they had put him on intravenous feeding. However, because he was in a Catholic hospital, they had wanted to institute a more aggressive measure by implanting a feeding tube to directly access his stomach. A feeding tube is a bigger step to keep the patient alive by artificial means.

As Don's agent, I was able to decline this measure. I had seen the intelligence of the body at work in hospice. The body knows when it wants and needs food. A feeding tube overrides the body's ability to know and communicate hunger on its own.

A Will is necessary to make sure your assets are probated and distributed to the people you want them to go to. To avoid probate, all assets must be titled in a trust, or the assets must each have designated beneficiaries. It is good to have a physical copy of any beneficiary designation prepared by your partner; that way, after your partner's death, you know and can demonstrate that you are the beneficiary. By having a copy of the designation, you will be able to submit a death certificate for release of the asset directly to you.

In the case of one client I worked with, a woman had left $4 million to the Salvation Army, but had changed the designation later to her two nieces. The actual photocopy of the document for her nieces was destroyed in the 9/11 attack on the World Trade Center. The bank only had an old copy of the designation on file that listed the Salvation Army as the sole beneficiary. The nieces were left out of the inheritance.

The ease with which estate cases unfold depends on whether certain details have been given attention—and in a crisis, it is easy to disregard such detail. The Power of Attorney for Property documents in writing who can be trusted to make decisions regarding your finances. In my own situation, Don and I had failed to have the proper number of witnesses sign his Power of

Attorney for Property, which ultimately prevented me from having access to liquid funds in Don's account. I was able to sort out this discrepancy, but this small oversight was particularly stressful during that chaotic time.

While these legal documents are important, the simple task of bill-paying can be crucial. I worked on another case in which a man who had a wife and three children let his life insurance premiums go unpaid for the last three months before he died. When he died, the family was unable to receive $300,000 in life insurance, although he had been paying the premiums for fifteen years. The notices of premium suspension had been unheeded because bills were not being tended to during his illness. The young, stay-at-home mother faced going to work at a minimum-wage job to support her children.

Whether you complete the paperwork on your own or hire a lawyer, it is important that everything is filled out correctly so that the documents are valid in the eyes of the law. It also helps to make sure someone is available to pay attention to bill paying and to maintenance of accounts so nothing lapses.

The insensitivities of the medical system can challenge the sanity of even the most calm and centered individual. The month after Don died, I kept getting voicemail messages from the cardiologist's office and letters in the mail saying Don had missed his scheduled appointment, and that by not showing up he was risking his opportunity to continue seeing the doctor. Don was dead, but the office kept leaving messages insinuating he was being irresponsible regarding his health and his relationship with his medical providers.

A robotic communication system had obviously reduced Don to a mere name in a computer file. However, the doctors behind the communication were as disconnected from the patient and as clueless to his status as the messages. The cardiologists focused predominantly on surgery and pharmaceuticals. They had subtly perpetuated a fear that if their protocol was not followed, there was no chance of healing.

In Don's crisis, I experienced firsthand the limitations of this belief system. Furthermore, I saw how compelling it is for a patient to adopt a cardiologist's drug protocol (oftentimes blindly), when all other integrative care options are dismissed by the doctor. This is not about condemning the medical system—it is about raising our own mind-body awareness and knowing about an increasing array of integrative options such as homeopathy, naturopathy, Chinese medicine, and energy medicine, to name a few.

A friend introduced me to a Chinese doctor who had been originally trained and had formerly practiced in the medical world as a traditional Western allopathic physician. His insights about the medical field reflect my own mixed feelings. He has become a valued consultant, offering patients wisdom and guidance when they choose and become involved in the allopathic model. He encourages patients to trust and listen to their own body, and teaches them how to seek out and to advocate for remedies and methods that they believe might complement their allopathic protocol.

Asking questions can lessen fear and frustration. Medical professionals are busy charting patient statistics all the time, because of liability and regulations. They end up building a database of detailed information, but they may not stay in touch with the body and the being of the patient. You are the best advocate to be the eyes and ears for your loved one. You also have permission, if you are the person's authorized agent, to tap into the charted database, which will help keep you informed about what's going on.

While you are in the hospital for hours and hours, know that you can ask to see the records and become more familiar with the procedures that are taking place. You can know exactly what drugs are administered, and in what dosages. You can see how their vitals are responding and what kind of progress has been made—if any. Charts are not particularly fun to read, but they are available, and they can show you a snapshot you can respond to.

At this point, you might be thinking, *What if I forget something?* It may seem as if there are too many moving pieces to keep track of. Who's to say something won't slip through the cracks?

Yes, it is important to have your affairs in order, but the simple truth is that there's no guarantee everything will go the way you want, no matter how well you prepare. We all have human aspects, and that means we sometimes overlook things. Look at me—I had years and years of experience in dealing with death and dying, and I still forgot key details. But you know what? If you remain open and receptive as you go along, life has a way of correcting itself.

I have always believed that if I stay "tuned in" and allow events to unfold, I will be guided toward what is true for me. The human body is always working toward a state of balance; the same is true of life in general. So it's okay if you forget something, or if a detail falls through the cracks. The universe has your back.

Right around the time I had my experience with my son, Connor, naming "God" as one of the sounds in the summer night, I was studying a book called *A Course in Miracles*. The book talks a lot about the Holy Spirit. I was raised Catholic and I was rebelling against all those Catholic ideas, but this book isn't about Catholicism. It isn't about dogmatic beliefs; rather, it's about perception.

The miracle is that, if you call on the Holy Spirit, you will receive a change in perception. Suddenly, the Holy Spirit became an icon I could relate to. And whenever I asked the Holy Spirit, I would get a change in perception. If I was angry with someone—change in perception. If I had lost something—change in perception, and then I'd often find the lost item or get over it. Calling on the Holy Spirit was a simple, powerful tool.

During the days when Don was in hospice and in a coma, I desperately needed a change in perception. Despairing, I said out loud, "God, please shift me out of my fear. I need a sign to boost my spirits." Later, on the way to the hospital, I drove up behind an old VW van with a spray-painted mural; on the back window, in big letters, was the phrase, "The Holy Spirit is with you." And just like that, I was infused with a sense of peace.

Now that I have a three-year-old grandson, I've probably seen the movie *Finding Nemo* at least 200 times. It's the only movie I own, so we watch it over and over again. I once heard that you can tell a great painting if, every time you look at it, you see something new. Silly as it might sound, *Finding Nemo* is one of the best paintings I've ever seen.

The movie is about a fish named Marlin, who helplessly watches his son Nemo, being scooped up by a scuba diver. Marlin immediately sets out on a journey to find him and along the way picks up a friend (and comic relief), Dory. In the cartoon, Marlin keeps thinking something bad is going to happen, and so he keeps trying to cover himself, which inevitably leads to him beating himself over the head, lamenting that he wasn't there for Nemo. Every situation reflects his anxiety over what might go wrong next.

Marlin and Dory go through many escapades in the ocean. At one point, they get swallowed by a giant whale. Certain that this is the end, Marlin hangs onto the side of the whale's mouth in fear. Dory tells Marlin she hears the whale saying, "It's time to let go!"

"But how do you know something bad won't happen?" Marlin asks.

"I don't!" Dory says as she's whisked away. Finally, Marlin lets go, they're blown out through the whale's spout and are back swimming in the ocean.

Life is a lot like *Finding Nemo.* It's easy to get caught up in what we think we did wrong, or what we think might go wrong, but in the end, we have to let go. All kinds of things occur. Often, events are different from what we have planned or imagined. That is life. That was Marlin's journey, and it is ours as well. We are never going to make a correct decision every time. But if each of us has the willingness to listen, trust, and to let go—to let the whale blow us forward—only then do we have the chance of swimming freely onward in the great sea of life.

EPILOGUE

Maybe in this great sea of life, we are all on a journey into Oneness, to which the Real People alluded. In these pages I have shared my story of that journey, which may be very different from your own. In sharing our stories as human beings, we have an amazing capacity to learn from each other's unique experiences. We are sentient beings. In witnessing and being witnessed, we feel connection. We heal.

Somewhere along the way, I have become an observer. I became aware of my search for definition and my desire to know how to handle life and death. I started out with a belief there was a right way, an explanation, an answer for this and for that. As I was graced with wise, spiritual teachers, I looked to them to point the way to a seamless path. Instead, I kept finding myself in the realm of the unknown and the uncomfortable. This was a space where the unspoken reigned. I began to perceive how differently I learned without the plethora of words spoken or written.

For instance, in each hospice case, there was no booklet to guide me. There was no ideal way to assist someone in the dying process. I often felt awkward, not sure of myself. However, in acknowledging whatever thoughts and feelings came up inside of me, a doorway opened. I could then lean away from any fixed concept of how death should be, or what communication should look like, and be open to what was true for the patient in that moment in their own journey. Sometimes, the end of life was peaceful, and sometimes it was very messy.

In the case of the hospice patient Anna, a DNR order (Do-Not-Resuscitate: see Appendix Legal) was in place, but a nurse disregarded it. Anna's body was shocked back into recovery against her wishes. However, this unexpectedly gave her estranged son extra time in which to arrive at the hospital and ask her for forgiveness before she passed.

In hindsight, the seamless path is really a series of doors, one opening into another and another. And with the crossing of each threshold, a new awareness comes as you step through. There is no language. In this way, life becomes a dance of listening to the nuances. Listening for what is unspoken. You begin aligning with the rhythm of life itself instead of searching for one door with a foolproof set of instructions.

In Don's case, every day of his medical crisis was another threshold to the unknown. The choices were never cut and dried. However, I wanted my steps to be flawless. I wanted to count the music so I didn't miss a beat. And yet I was pulled into the string of a thousand moments that became a melody all its own. In the final moments, I was blessed with a deep sense of communion.

With Alan and with other children in Suzy Miller's movement, known as "Awesomism," this deep sense of communion is available. It was Riley, (the four-year-old who set Suzy on her own path into the unknown) whose words have stayed with me. After being non-verbal since birth, his first written words were: "Advance the magic!" The children are here telling us and showing us how the magic of Oneness is available to each and every one of us. They purposefully reflect to us any layers that keep us separate. They ask us to show up and to show them who we really are.

As I have learned from the children, Don's death taught me firsthand how our journey into Oneness doesn't have to be about adopting a spiritual path or integrating our concepts about science and religion. Don lived with a kindness and caring that seemed easy for him. He walked through life with an open heart. His path was simple, unspoken.

It was just Don being Don.

APPENDIX

Checklist for Chapter 9

Medical:

• Run through calling health insurance company to ensure you have access to all information.

• Review health insurance policy and network providers.

Financial:

• Make friends with your banker.

• Ensure you and your partner have access to each other's accounts through Power of Attorney for Property or Joint Tenancy.

• Go over any shared accounts to check that you are either:

  1. Named as beneficiaries on each other's accounts .

  2. Designated as POD –"Payable on Death."

  3. Designated as TOD – "Transfer on Death."

4. JTWROS –Titled as Joint Tenants with Right of Survivorship.

- Keep a list of any accounts and put relevant documents (bank and brokerage accounts, home ownership documents, insurance policies, etc.) in a lockbox.

Legal:

- *Obtain a Power of Attorney for Healthcare:* Null and void upon death of principal.

- *Obtain a Power of Attorney for Property:* Null and void upon death of principal.

- *Obtain a Will:* Goes into effect at death and assets must be probated.

- *A trust is optional:* Usually costs several thousand dollars to be set up by a lawyer. It transfers assets titled in the trust to the heirs without going through probate. In addition to preparing a trust document, make sure the lawyer re-titles all the assets in the name of the trust in order for them to be distributed without going through probate. Designating beneficiaries on your accounts is a way to transfer assets outside of probate court without a trust. Simple probate usually costs several thousand dollars.

- *Keep document originals in a safe place:* Destroy any outdated documents.

- *Know the meaning of a DNR or Do-Not-Resuscitate order before signing it:* It is not an end-of-life directive that says you don't want extraordinary measures to keep you alive in the event you are dying. It is a very literal order that means you want to die at any moment without any medical intervention. DNR orders are appropriate for persons in the end stages of dying or in hospice care who have chosen to end aggressive treatment.

In the Hospital:

- Ask questions.

- Know you have access to the patient's charts.

- Keep any valuables in a secure place.

Don and I

That's Don!

Balbir at our Wedding

Baron – the Mystic Dog

Baron Walking Don

CPSIA information can be obtained
at www.ICGtesting.com
Printed in the USA
FSOW03n1732080316
17800FS

9 780692 654651